ATHEIST YOGA

Anton Drake

Puragreen Productions LLC

A Puragreen Productions LLC Publication

Copyright © 2013 by Anton Drake

All rights reserved.

No part of this book may be reproduced in any form or by any means, electronic or mechanical, including photocopying, recording or by any information storage or retrieval system, without permission in writing from the publisher or author.

ISBN 978-0-9831502-3-7

Disclaimer

This book is intended for educational purposes only. The information, techniques, ideas and suggestions in this book are not intended as a substitute for professional medical advice. Always consult your physician or health care professional before performing any new exercise or fitness routine. Any application of the techniques, ideas, and suggestions in this book is at the reader's sole discretion and risk. Some of the exercises described in this book may be too strenuous for some people, and the reader should consult their health practitioner before engaging in them. The editors, authors and or publishers of this book make no warranty of any kind about the contents of this book or any of the information contained in it. Neither the author nor the publisher shall be liable or responsible for any injury, damage or loss allegedly arising, either directly or indirectly, from any of the information, techniques or suggestions contained within this book.

Contents

1. Midnight, Los Angeles	1
2. Atheism and Yoga	5
3. Bodily Reflection	11
4. Hollywood	17
5. Materialism	21
6. Ego, Amigo	29
7. El Segundo	39
8. Hatha Yoga	43
9. Asana	51
10. The Core	63
11. Pranayama	75
12. Las Vegas	89
13. Kundalini & the Chakras	93
14. Sexuality and Yoga	127
15. Yogic Sex	143
16. Beverly Hills	151
17. Meditation Theory	157
18. Meditation Tactics	165
Bibliography	181

1

MIDNIGHT, LOS ANGELES

I woke up in the back of a darkened yoga studio, sitting on the floor Indian style, my head hanging forward heavily. The glowing red numbers on the far wall said it was 12:30AM; the only other light in the room was a beam of powdery L.A. Moon-milk slicing in from above the shutters. Two hours earlier I had sat down in this corner after class, blocking out the sounds of friendly banter and dispersal and craving just a few more minutes of translucent honeyed solitude. Now, on the other side of sleep, the mirrored walls around me seemed to open into caves of jungle shadows; I rubbed my eyes awake and realized suddenly that I was not alone, that someone was sitting next to me in the darkness. My body jolted with a reflexive adrenal sniff, splashing sparkly pixels across my retinas. She stirred, lifting up her long neck and slowly opening her eyes, languidly swinging her head around toward me, slowly; she leaned in to my face, her eyes appearing black and shiny in the darkness.

'It's a good night for meditation,' she said in a casual tone. Her voice was emotionless and flat, but flavored with a smooth Spanish accent and a noticeable tenor of sophistication. I had seen her in class that night, lean and unadorned, apparently a friend of the teacher; now she sat, wound carelessly into a relaxed lotus posture next to me, her long black hair glistening like oil over the fluid curves of her shoulders. I sat silent for a couple seconds; I had been meditating intensely, and my spine still felt hot, bound up with an achy, languid bliss, which seemed to fill with icy cold air each time I breathed in; my jaw felt thick, and a pleasantly fevered scratched-itch sensation seemed to ooze down slowly from the center of my brain, pulling up my cheekbones and dripping down into my upper canines. My eyes steadied and cooled as I looked at her, mutely; she looked back, studying me. With a quick gesture of her tongue she languidly unwound her legs and rose to her feet, straightening and stretching herself upward and exhaling sharply. Then she dropped down all at once, as if from the ceiling, landing directly in front of me as she recrossed her legs so that her knees were just touching mine. I felt the cool fingers of her left hand slide smoothly around my neck with a serpentine slowness, as she pulled me all the way forward, until our heads were pressing hard together. She twisted and ground her forehead into mine, luxuriously, the way a cat might; I could feel a tingle of warm vanilla in my lungs.

'There's something I want to... tell you,' she whispered, in a slow, almost subsonic hiss. My eyes rolled upward with a shudder of serene contentment toward our conjoined foreheads. She slid her hand along to my shoulder, then tapped me backward with a sisterly nudge; her legs cinched deeper around each other as she sat up straighter, seeming to sway imperceptibly as I leveled and refocused my eyes on her. For a long, still moment, it felt as if a gulf of emptiness was expanding the distance between us; her body seemed solid and silent, firmly rooted into the floor as if it was made of heavy onyx, radiating like the black center of an eclipse. My eyes suddenly felt unbearably tired and I closed them, almost in annoyance, and felt myself instantly pulled down into a blue-black undercurrent of meditation below, my thoughts dissolving.

'Hey,' she said. 'I, want, to, tell, you, something...' She firmly punctuated each syllable with a poke of her finger down into the top of my thigh. I opened my eyes again to see her smiling toothily and laughing huskily to herself. For some reason I imagined her drinking coffee on the veranda of a marbled South American palace somewhere, surrounded by rainforest jungle.

'What,' I said. Her eyebrows lowered into a dark frown and she glared at me intently, her eyes laying into mine with an unrelenting gravity; I stared back as long as I could, then burst out laughing, my dreaminess splintered into irretrievably sharp edges. She smiled, somewhat pleased with herself.

'Let's go to Hollywood and get some Thai food,' she said.

2

ATHEISM AND YOGA

The practice of yoga is capable of generating deep states of inward meditative absorption and physical relaxation. Its techniques can open up pathways of blissfully stress-free repose, melting through physical and mental tension from the inside, and bathing the psyche in the healing waters of the unconscious mind. The practice of yoga is also a method of generating profound mental concentration, which can be used to develop precise control over the body, and to hone the mind toward a laser-like mental focus. The complete art of yoga lies at the nexus of these two polarities, where the hot morning Sun of intensely focused awareness and control, and the cold midnight Moon of calm relaxation and tranquil oblivion overlap, blending into cool and balanced equipoise.

Today, the stress relieving and anti-aging effects of yoga are well known, and are a major reason for yoga's surge in popularity; in general, however, the popular understanding of what yoga is barely scratches its surface. Correctly practiced, yoga is capable of unlocking and releasing deep, hidden layers of physical and mental tension; much of its effectiveness in combating and reversing the corrosive effects of aging, in fact, stems directly from the rejuvenating side effects of such rigorous and systematic relaxation. Removing the entrenched roadblocks of physical and emotional tension can unbind circulation and respiration, thus allowing the body to replenish and recharge itself while simultaneously soothing and relaxing the mind. Of course, there is far more to yoga than relaxation; however, yoga's advanced techniques for digging deep below the surface of the outward person in order to untangle and resolve the physical and unconscious roots of stress are so comprehensive and so profoundly effective that their value simply cannot be overestimated.

One of the key elements for mastering yoga lies in understanding that every technique is a way of relating to yourself. From this it follows that the essence of the art is always to be found in its general principles, rather than in any accumulation of meticulous detail or arcane technical intricacy, simply because being good at yoga is something that you *are,* and not something external that can be gotten by following or mimicking a repetitious pattern or sequence. And as useful as external techniques and exercises may be, when skill in yoga increases it will always be manifested within the reflective nature of one's own self, and nowhere else. Attributes such as balance, breath control, spinal-extension, body-awareness and mental focus can only be developed from the inside out, and are vastly more significant than, for example, the way one holds one's thumb and forefinger. Yoga is subjective and reflective in its deepest essence, a practice altogether different from, for example, dance, which is closer to an outward language of physical movement and expression. In hatha yoga, by contrast, each technique is a progression inward toward greater self-awareness for its own sake, and it this inner quality of absorption and reflectivity, how the technique is perceived and understood internally, that is actually far more important than its outward expression. This kind of understanding has to be worked out on an individual level, and can only be gained from determined and solitary practice. In this, it is always key to remember that yoga is a living art, which has been constantly evolving for many thousands of years; it is left to each individual practitioner to solve its puzzles, and to avoid its peculiar dangers and pitfalls.

Viewed in its proper context, the art of yoga can be seen to be something that is fully flexible and alive and capable of evolving further as it progresses into the future; this open-ended and evolving quality of yoga is one of the main reasons that it is so thoroughly compatible with atheism and materialism. It is also one of the reasons that atheism can be a real advantage in the practice of yoga, since atheism frees one from the burden and internal dissonance of religious belief and allows one to proceed forward in meditative practice with an open mind, devoid of any prefabricated 'spiritual' or metaphysical expectations and without any need to expend mental energy guarding against the pestering intrusion of doubt—which is, after all, the voice of one's own intellect. Atheists, in fact, are free to indulge in doubt to the utmost degree, even to the point of approaching the entire process of meditation from a stance of epistemological uncertainty, embracing an entire subjective universe of doubt and enjoying the luxury of seeing everything through the clear eyes of godlessness and unbelief.

In pursuing the objectives of yoga and meditation, one of the toughest obstacles is the internal resistance of psychological repression, which can turn the mind against itself by literally blocking and distorting consciousness. While this may in a sense be a natural outgrowth of our social instincts and a necessary function of a healthy Ego, in the process of meditation it is an obstacle, since meditation requires above all that one see oneself clearly and honestly. Such inner transparency is always at odds with the forces of psychological repression, especially those engines of repression fueled by phantom fears and deeply ingrained false beliefs; deep meditative relaxation thrives best when the deep snarls and emotional conflicts that hinder and constrain one's self-image can be rooted out and untangled, allowing for greater conscious control of reflexive stress responses and thereby reducing one's overall levels of tension and stress, allowing for even further progress in meditation and yoga.

True meditation never involves fighting with one's own mind, or struggling to suppress 'bad' thoughts with 'good' ones. Meditation does require, however, honest self-trust and a genuine sense of self-acceptance, which allows the mind to be at peace and to come more fully into alignment with itself. Freedom from religion makes this process easier, because religious belief, to the extent that it is an extension of external social norms and suggests a kind of divine inner surveillance, fosters self-repression almost by its very nature. Forcing oneself to believe in something that does not actually exist, especially on the assumption that any failure to so believe might prove perilously sinful, can lead to a sort of bunker-mentality where the mind, under continual pressure to quickly 'shout down' any internal doubt or dissent, cannot easily look at itself for fear that some unsanctioned thought or feeling might sneak through and stain it with guilt. This can wind up generating additional layers of psychological repression, in the form of continual pious chatter or cant, which distance one even further from the serene inner gardens of meditation.

For a meditator, the problem with trying to conform to a prefabricated religious or spiritual conception of reality is that it is inherently self-limiting, requiring a continual inhibition of the intellect. Free and unrestricted thought leads to questions, and questions lead to doubts; doubts in their turn can impose a considerable cost upon those who are clinging to faith, because of the time, energy and effort required to rationalize them away. The ultimate cost, however, of setting fixed boundaries for one's introspective reasoning is that, in time, the intellect is forced to warp itself so that it always leans subconsciously away from question and doubt toward whatever tends to grease the tracks of smooth and uninterrupted belief. Thus, unquestioning faith in an omniscient and omnipresent God or Supreme Being can be a true obstacle to the practice of yoga and meditation, setting up a buffer that literally separates one from one's self and burdens the mind with mountains of dissonance and metaphysical presupposition, constantly blurring the reality of personal experience. On the other hand, if one is free from the overhead of maintaining a rigid structure of spiritual faith things are much easier; the mind and the intellect can function naturally without filters or censors, thus allowing for the peaceful mental clarity so precious to the art of meditation.

3

BODILY REFLECTION

'Yoga means concentration.' – Swami Hariharananda Aranya, Yoga Philosophy of Patanjali

Whether the techniques of yoga are viewed as a system for preparing the body and the mind for meditation or as the outward manifestation of meditation, meditation is unquestionably the heart of yoga, and all forms of yoga stem directly from it in one way or another. Hatha yoga techniques such as breath control capitalize on what is ultimately the purely physical nature of the psyche itself by tapping directly into the inseparable unity of the body and the mind and altering consciousness through physical control. Yogic breath control is thus a direct pathway for the mind to control itself, an ability undoubtedly evolved through the practice of meditation. This kind of meditative self-control, which works to affect changes in the mind directly through the physiology of the body, is a quintessential characteristic of yoga practice, rooted in a deeply intuitive understanding of the essentially material nature of consciousness.

Thoughts, memories and fantasies, when viewed subjectively from inside of consciousness, are certainly made of something much different than the meat, blood and bone of corporeal existence; objectively, however, the mind and all of its contents are generated by the neuronal structure of the living physical brain. Naturally, this also implies that the mind cannot exist without the body; just as when a computer is unplugged the electronic structure of its dynamically stored data instantaneously vanishes from its memory modules, or RAM, the death of the physical body results in the absolute and irretrievable loss of the individual psyche into nonexistence. Interestingly, then, what is often fancifully called the 'mind-body connection' must actually be a corollary of scientific materialism; the mind not only shares the most intimate possible connection with the body, but a fundamental identity as well. Paradoxically, when viewed subjectively from the inside the physical body is itself only perceived as a reflection in the mind, a mental image in consciousness always one step removed from direct self-perception. In yoga meditation, the objective is to refine and deepen this reflective awareness of self and to even go beyond it, into the unconscious and the purely physical—to get 'down to the metal' of the hardwired boundaries of knowing and awareness and explore the primal low-level self-awareness native to the physical organism of the body itself. Ironically, it is monist materialism itself that provides a yoga practitioner with the proper understanding with which to pursue the attainment of yogic body-control and meditative mental equilibrium, and it is atheism that can allow a practitioner the inner freedom to fearlessly seek the serene emptiness of profound meditation. Such an approach to meditation is certainly not without precedent; the classical yoga philosophy of Patanjali was actually derived directly from Samkhya, an atheistic system of thought that is the oldest of the six major schools of Indian Vedic philosophy. Dating back more than 2,500 years, Samkhya presents a dualistic conception of the universe consisting of two separate planes of reality, the plane of physical matter and the plane of subjective consciousness; one of the strikingly modern features of Samkhya philosophy is that it actually describes the mind as being part of the physical, material plane of reality.

Properly understood, the body-control techniques of hatha yoga are also techniques for concentrating and stilling the mind; in working to control the body with intense mental focus and absorption, the mind also gains a handle on itself; it gradually learns to hold itself in greater stillness and repose, mirroring the outward stillness and balance of the body. In the practice of yoga the most intimate conception of one's own body, the ragdoll homunculus at the center of the body's kinesthetic sense organs and controllers and its understanding of its extended physical self, gains in control and precision, continually refining and deepening its connections to the body and eventually learning to relax completely into the stillness of meditation, translating the supple emptiness of inner tranquility into its physical equivalent. Meditative stillness and concentration is integral to hatha yoga, enabling a practitioner to focus awareness completely onto the physical body, mentally 'merging,' so to speak, with a position or technique, as the mind becomes one-pointed in controlling the body. The second aphorism of Patanjali's Yoga Sutras can be translated as 'yoga is the stilling of the thought-waves of the mind'; this elusive quality of mental stillness and solid equipoise is a primary element of meditation, which is fully expressed in the solidity and balance of a properly performed hatha yoga pose, that peculiar stone-Buddha quality the body assumes as it mirrors the lucid tranquility of the mind in meditation.

A crucial attribute in all of this is an unrestricted sense of mental-freedom, an unconditional sense of self-ownership and self-love that feels itself worthy to interpret and possess the full quantum of its own awareness, reason and intuition. To attain the yogic ability to descend into thought-free meditation at will the mind must first of all possess the freedom to think about absolutely anything without restriction, without guilt and without exception; a certain inner confidence and command of self is necessary if the mind will seek to pursue the simple quiet of inner stillness and equanimity. This kind of mental-freedom stands in stark contrast to its opposite, which is embodied by the mind completely ruled by faith in an omnipresent God and finds itself obliged to cringe inwardly in submission before this nebulous imaginary overlord at all times, consigned to perpetual distrust of its own unguarded and spontaneous thoughts, and unquestioning in its belief that something higher is always present, watching and judging it. The ultimate caricature of this type as described in fiction is the self-flagellating monk, who literally whips himself bloody, beating back the impulses of his psyche like an unruly beast of burden for the sake of pleasing his imaginary master and who then subsequently projects his profound distrust of self outward onto humanity, envisioning the entire world as hopelessly infected by evil and sin. For such a mind, meditative inner stillness is simply intolerable and therefore not a suitable goal; not only because meditation is likely to release torrents of repressed psychological ugliness but also because, from a pious perspective, the very idea of self-possession and quiet authenticity is in itself arrogant and therefore disrespectful. Real meditation, however, requires that the mind must be its own master; by contrast, the mind that is trapped into imagining an all-powerful and divine king looking over its shoulder at every instant, constantly ready to reward or punish, occupies the position of a slave or prisoner and possesses no such dominion over itself, and therefore no ability to truly *meditate* on itself. While it may at times seem to evince an outward pride in religious conformity or identity, inwardly it cannot acknowledge itself or grant itself even the slightest autonomy, and must willingly consign itself to cringe, grovel and ceaselessly apologize before its unseen inner supervisor.

That the techniques of yoga are so easily reframed into the context of explicit atheism is largely due to the fact that yoga is at its core such a profoundly personal practice, which places a fundamental emphasis on introspection and self-mastery. Of course, in various traditions the practice of yoga has often been melded with religious faith or devotion to God in one form or another; Patanjali's classical yoga philosophy, in fact, makes fundamentally the same assumption as Buddhism, which is that the mind and the self are at bottom identical with a Supreme Being, and that all other forms of perception and cognition are essentially nothing more than forms of self-delusion. According to this view, reaching the 'absolute' within oneself necessitates the somewhat wrenching psychological austerity of completely overcoming one's sense of personal agency or 'doership' and permanently recasting the Ego and the individual personality as nothing more than pernicious obstacles on the path to enlightenment, which must be broken down, overthrown and dissolved. Such an approach assumes that since 'God' exists inside of you all that is required to reach enlightenment is for 'you' to get out of the way; in other words, once you as an individual have ceased to exist, 'enlightenment' will be attained. An atheistic practice of yoga differs radically from this, in that it completely lacks faith in any kind of God or Supreme Being and consequently requires no convoluted metaphysical gymnastics to make sense out of itself; the mind exists and God does not, and therefore the proper direction of meditation is either inward toward consciousness and the self, or outward toward external objects, which in a sense amounts to the same thing since external objects are always perceived within the subjective domain of consciousness, perception and understanding and nowhere else. All of the fundamental techniques of yoga are entirely compatible with atheism and materialism, assuming that one always takes the approach of adapting what is useful and discarding everything else. Yoga lends itself to this interpretation quite naturally, since the material value of its techniques is always derived solely from their physical and mental effects, which are essentially indifferent to all other considerations. One can meditate perfectly well, for example, while focusing the mind on something as mundane as the vastness of our local star system, or the infinite depths of cosmic space and time.

4

HOLLYWOOD

I savored another bite of tofu spring roll dipped in Thai curry as she chewed her way somewhat viciously through a piece of sautéed calamari.

'At some point I just realized that I'd always been an atheist,' she said. 'I'd just always been fighting it, fighting myself. Then one day I got it together and just made the decision to let go; I was scared, thrilled, you know; like this is really happening, this is the moment I'm going to stop believing. And then I did, and, of course, nothing happened. I just kind of exhaled, you know, and everything was exactly the same. And then after a while things somehow began getting clearer, I could see things more clearly, even in a physical sense. Eventually I just wanted more and more, because every time I found another piece of faith in myself and rooted it out that feeling got even better.'

'This curry is so good,' I said. 'Unreal.'

'I think as far back as I can remember, I'd always been trying to find a way to believe in God, to make myself believe. Deep down I think I felt that if I ever stopped believing, even for a second, I'd instantly be sucked down into eternal damnation. As if my whole life had been leading up to that one moment when I might finally lose my faith, and then boom! That's it, eternal damnation, your soul is devoured. But after I got free from believing, I realized I'd been living my whole life inside a giant superstition.'

'It is outlandishly weird,' I said. 'At least we get to see it though. That's something.'

'Sometimes I think it's like a huge spider sucked onto the back of the entire human species,' she said, 'You know, one thing I had found in meditation is that sometimes it was like one side of my brain was thinking logically in words, but the other side was kind of mute, even though it was just as strong, just as present, just as much a part of me. So for instance maybe I'd tell myself that, hey, no way am I gonna eat some chocolate cake; but then I turn around and there's a piece of chocolate cake in my mouth. How did that happen? And it's like this mute donkey side of myself, like what the hell, nobody mentioned to me that we weren't having cake. And I feel like maybe that's where my fear of not believing always was; like maybe somebody told me when I was a baby that if you ever stop believing then you'll die, forever. Eternal death. And so this mute donkey side of myself can't understand any words, but it understood *that*, it *remembered that*; so now you can't make sense to it, you can't reason with it, you can't even talk to it, because for one thing you don't even know it's there, but also because deep down all it has is a feeling, a feeling that if it doesn't believe it will actually die. Then, ok, one day it really dawns on you that everything was fake, there is no Santa Klaus. Everything you believed in was a story. And you just let go and stop believing. And it's scary at first, you know, because suddenly you feel like there's nothing underneath you, but then you realize there was never anything underneath you.'

'After college I was super into spirituality,' I said. 'Guru worship, deities, Buddhas, Boddhisattvas, inner transcendence, everything. I was seeing God everywhere, you know? I'd literally bow down to a stick of incense. And then I found Freud. I got so obsessed with Freud, after a while, everyday, all the time, I was always thinking about the Unconscious. Everything that happened, I'd always think "what does it mean," you know? Where did it come from? What part of the mind. How deep does it go. And it's amazing because it's always there, and the more you look the more of it you find. And of course I was still meditating all the time. Then I found atheism. Now, I mean if you ask me, atheism should be its own branch of science.'

'Freud,' she smiled. 'I mean maybe we could say that Freud was the greatest mystic in history. But who the hell even knows what mystic means? It's meaningless. But Freud actually found something... Of course hardly anybody ever talks about this, but Freud's discovery of the Unconscious changed everything. All those scholars and theologians had been living on top of an iceberg for ten thousand years, arguing about how many angels could fit on the head of a pin or whatever, and then Freud comes along and points out that ninety-nine percent of everything is existing underneath and outside of everyone's awareness. And oops, no one had ever mentioned that before, or wrote that down before, because nobody knew; in all of history, nobody, and I mean nobody, had ever been capable of conceptualizing that. In retrospect, it's maybe even more devastating than Darwin.'

'Well, to be fair, maybe for a hundred years there were others getting close,' I said. 'Hume, for example,

Schopenhauer, Nietzsche, they were all pushing up against it. And Darwin obviously influenced Freud.'

'Speaking of Freud, what I like to do sometimes is just watch TV for the commercials,' she said. 'Super slow motion, frame by frame... Beer, soda, underwear... dog food, deodorant, trash bags, makeup. Just the commercials, one frame at a time in super HD. I love it. All the body language, the posturing, the urgency, the sexual excitement; the bulging muscles and all those futuristic cars with their pulsating digital dashboards; the flowing infinite golden hair, the moist lips and the tight buns, the exploding action heroes covered in tar. The square yards with perfect lawns and the pop stars with the luminescent blue Venus flytrap eyes, a foot wide on my flat-screen. I mean sometimes... I mean honestly where are you going to find better stuff these days? It's like a glowing, pulsating art gallery right there in your living room. And it's all so Freudian now too, which gives it this dangerous, lurid edge, like it's desperately trying to claw at your brain from inside the screen. And some of the shows... I mean I think you've gotta admit TV is pretty amazing these days.'

'Turned to stone by the digital Medusa,' I said, grinning.

'Yeah I hardly think so,' she snickered, biting into a mouthful of squid tentacles.

5

MATERIALISM

Materialism accepts as fact the modest assertion that the universe is real and exists as an objective reality, entirely independent of human consciousness and perception. And since humans exist within this real and objective universe of energy and matter it therefore follows that humans are also objectively real and exist at some level as objects outside of their own subjective self-awareness. One way that we know the universe is real is because wherever the tools of scientific exploration have managed to scratch into the substance of objective reality, progressively deeper layers of structural complexity and being have been revealed, which have in turn unfailingly turned out to be reconcilable with everything that science has previously discovered about the world; the vast and expanding interlocking complexity of scientific understanding and empirical knowledge thus renders absurdly improbable any conception of the universe as being nothing more than some kind of dreamlike illusion or mental projection. Therefore, while there is certainly a vast difference between subjective and objective reality—that is to say, between one's internal mental perception of the universe and raw external reality—the simple fact is that the universe is real and exists in a material sense.

While the idea that the universe is 'real' might seem trivial, it is actually diametrically opposed to, for example,

Buddhist metaphysical ideas about existence, which view the universe as fundamentally *unreal*—an illusory projection of the mind created through ignorance of its own 'transcendent' nature, which separates it from the pure reality of a Supreme Being or supreme consciousness. Buddhism and other idealist systems are ultimately based on the premise that the universe we occupy is actually a purely subjective mental projection that would cease to exist in the absence of individual consciousness; in this view reality exists as a kind of dream, created and mediated by the power of a Supreme Being and having scope only within the solipsistic universe of each individual mind. Such belief systems are, again, diametrically opposed to materialism and realism; interestingly, it is precisely this point that often gets misinterpreted or misrepresented in spiritual writings and lectures: one way this occurs is when philosophical materialism is intentionally conflated with economic materialism, that is, with the belief that the acquisition of material goods and wealth should be the main objective in life. Economic materialism might well be criticized as being spiritually vacuous or low and representing the epitome of narcissistic greed and selfishness; in many 'spiritual' works however, the underlying sneer is actually directed at materialistic monism and realism—the idea that the world is a real place made of matter and energy, rather than an illusory mystical dream or mental projection. Many gurus, in fact, ostentatiously flaunt wealth and luxury precisely to make the point that all difference in material circumstance is nothing more than illusion; this is frequently pointed to by skeptics as being hypocritical but is in fact a classic theme of mysticism. Of course, all systems of mystical philosophy fall apart once realism and materialism are accepted; ironically, however, part of mysticism's underlying charm has always been the hint that it might offer the keys to magical prosperity—the tangible examples of which are usually not much more than the fruits of one pyramid scam or another. In any case, confusing greed or consumerism with philosophical materialism is an obvious error; while many people may intuitively believe in a modicum of altruism and feel that purely selfish economic materialism is reprehensible, such a sentiment is clearly something vastly different from the belief that everything and everyone in the entire world is nothing more than an illusion—a worldview that could in practice potentially turn out to be even more profoundly selfish, destructive and nihilistic than an economic philosophy of raw greed.

The doctrine that every human person lives trapped within a 'wheel' of birth, death and reincarnation, tragically separated from a transcendent consciousness or 'Buddha-principle,' is rooted in the belief that the material universe is an illusion; according to this view, as individual consciousness gains in 'purity' and detachment and begins to approach 'transcendence' its belief in this illusory material world diminishes and it begins to acquire a proportional degree of power and mastery over it. In a similar way, one's good or bad deeds are said to affect the nature of reality itself and one's path through it, as guided by the unseen hand of Fate or karma, resulting in either more or less enjoyable personal circumstances depending on one's past actions; total 'liberation' or transcendence from this sticky and illusory web of life can only be achieved when one succeeds in 'awakening' from the dream of material existence altogether and is able to shed the individual Ego completely.

There are several immense problems with the view of reality just described; the first is that because consciousness is rooted in the physical body it is simply not possible for minds or 'souls' to exist without a body or to wander between bodies. And, if the metaphysical implications of evaluating, repackaging and rerouting a vast number of disembodied souls into new bodies and new lives through a process of 'transmigration' and reincarnation are considered, it becomes clear that such a state of affairs could not exist without a thoroughly omnipotent and omniscient creator God or Supreme Being of some kind—something that no evidence has ever existed for, and that is vastly improbable for a number of reasons. Perhaps the worst problem with this wheel of illusion and rebirth model, though, is that in the quest for 'liberation' it is ultimately the self-conscious human Ego or sense of I-ness that gets labeled as the chief obstacle to enlightenment and spiritual progress. Philosophically, if the world is presumed to be nothing more than an illusion within the mind and that mind is presumed to be nothing more than an impure veil concealing the true nature of spiritual reality, a grotesque devaluation of the Ego and the entire human psyche is unavoidable, as by definition these must necessarily be the source of all delusion, ignorance and 'spiritual' bondage. By contrast, however, since we begin from the assumption that the universe does in fact exist objectively within material reality and that there is no such thing as a 'Supreme Being' or God, any such philosophy or system of belief cannot help but appear absurdly nihilistic to us, undermining not only the ideals of human evolution, progress and technological advancement but the basis of reason and intelligence itself. After all, what real value can reason or human progress possibly have if the entire world is ultimately nothing more than a solipsistic delusion of the mind, a divine fishbowl of subjective dreams and 'spiritual tests'?

Ironically, proponents of religion frequently argue that it is actually materialism and atheism that are nihilistic, rather than the other way around. As a rule, the reasoning behind such arguments is never delved into very deeply; the argument generally just takes the form of the naked assertion that to not believe in God is tantamount to absolute nihilism. The unspoken logic however is that no objectively real or material universe actually exists, one's perception of reality existing only in the mind and not mapping onto anything real; therefore, since God has ostensibly created this illusion of reality and is, as a perfect being, more 'real' than anything else could possibly be, choosing to not believe in God is the same as choosing to believe in nothing, or nihilism. There are of course several strange things about this argument, starting with the idea that it is somehow possible to choose whether or not to 'believe' in something; the real backbone of the argument, though, lies in the tacit assumption that the world is not real in any material sense, and is in fact nothing more than a fool's gold of illusion concealing the real treasure of a divine or super-conscious realm or state of existence. This central assumption is in fact circular, however, because it begins with the idea of a God who is undefined and unknowable and exists within an inconceivable and transcendent domain outside of material existence, in some unspecified and undefined way, and from this premise arrives at the conclusion that the material universe must therefore be an illusion. In other words, based on the wild assumption that there exists, somehow, an 'immaterial' and transcendent mythical reality adjacent to and overlapping with our material universe, which is at the same time absolutely different and separate from it, the conclusion is reached that the material universe must therefore be an illusion and not objectively real. Thus, the instinctive and natural tendency toward believing in the urgent and material reality of the universe is dismissed as a perverse and nihilistic choice to intentionally embrace illusion over mystical or divine reality. Such an extreme devaluation of realism must, incidentally, also imply a certain disdain for empirical science as well; it can be assumed that any acceptance of science by the sincerely mystical must necessarily conceal within itself a measure of condescension, which cannot help but regard any empirical scientific exploration of this 'illusory' universe as a meaningless enterprise fueled by human vanity, Ego and delusion.

An interesting thing about the concept of God is that it cannot be clearly defined; one might well attempt to define it, in fact, in precisely these terms, as something indefinable and completely outside the scope of human perception and understanding. Gods and Supreme Beings are invariably described as being ultimately beyond all description and comprehension, entities that exist 'outside' of existence, so to speak, and therefore cannot be touched by human understanding. Linguistically, however, what does it mean to say that something 'exists' outside of the known physical universe, or is a priori 'unknowable'? At face value, such contortions seem to be nothing more than attempts to stretch language in order to assert that something nonexistent can or must exist, despite the fact that it can't even be coherently conceptualized; this essentially employs the verb 'to exist' in a novel and supremely ambiguous way, which is then rationalized with truckloads of metaphysical babble invariably leading back to the disappointingly barren shores of one ancient holy scripture or another. At bottom, however, all of these various explanations of 'transcendence' or 'transcendent being' rely upon the supposed 'existence' of an undefined and 'immaterial' void or domain beyond existence; on the level of the Unconscious, this almost certainly links back to the idea of actual nothingness, the inconceivable enigma of infinite nonexistence that is never more than a heartbeat away from anyone.

The distinction between the material universe and any hypothetical 'transcendent' or immaterial 'beyond' is a false one, for the simple reason that if such a transcendent realm were actually discovered to exist, it would then immediately be known to be part of the actual, existent, material universe. In this context, the word 'material,' in fact, seems to mean 'actual' or 'existent'; even the most infinitesimally small or subtle bits of matter, down to purely theoretical subatomic particles or strings, are acknowledged conceptually to belong to the material universe, as are even the most subtle forms of light and energy. The insistence, then, on a 'transcendent' and 'nonphysical' state of existence 'beyond' existence at bottom denies the reality of the material universe itself and in effect says that the only 'real' thing is God. This, however, leads right back to the same circularity, because the concepts of 'God' and 'transcendence' have only been explained as being unknowable and 'outside' of material existence; apart from the qualities of being unknowable, indefinable and untouched by the material universe, then, they are essentially undefined. And in the end, what does it actually mean to say that an unknowable, immaterial and indefinable object called God 'exists,' in an undefined way, in some unknowable realm entirely outside of the scope of existence?

Atheism, realism and materialism thus all converge on the foundational premise that the world, the universe and we ourselves all exist, objectively, whether we happen to be aware of it at any given moment or not. This is not to say, however, that there is not also a 'world' of subjective awareness within each individual, which usually maps more of less onto to a thin slice of objective reality according to the ways our organs of sense perception have evolved; this internal mental world of conscious experience, however, although existing as a kind of reflection in the eye of the subjective self, is also made of energy and matter, and is therefore itself part of the material universe as well. Consciousness, then, is objectively a part of material reality and not a portal 'out' of it; consciousness is also in a certain sense the deepest and most mysterious aspect of reality, that part of existence that we as humans are most intimately connected to, the quintessence of our individual life force and animal existence. Thus, in porting yoga over into the context of a godless and very real material universe, the object of meditation becomes consciousness itself, a deepened reflective awareness of the body and the psyche. Along these lines, something like an analogue for the object of 'transcendence' is found in the unconscious mind, the ever-present event horizon of human consciousness from which every thought arises and into which every thought disappears. The unconscious mind, which embodies a kind of organic wholeness linking consciousness to the physical body and to every other level of the psyche, offers the promise of expanding the frontiers of self-awareness and of surpassing the limitations of ordinary consciousness.

6

EGO, AMIGO

'I think, therefore I am.' – Rene Descartes

The mystic premise that material reality is nothing more than a pernicious illusion separating the mind from supreme consciousness or a Supreme Being contains within itself a hidden danger, which is that it not only relegates one's individual sense of self to the status of something unreal, but actually singles out the individual Ego as the primary obstacle to so-called enlightenment. In practice, this eventually boils down to the notion that a belief in the individual self is the primary obstacle to 'transcendence' or 'transformation': if everything is understood to be nothing more than a mystical illusion, and if one's own sense of individuality and Ego is regarded as nothing more than that which most viscerally binds one to the trappings of this illusion, the unavoidable logical implication is that the dissolution of the individual mind and personality is therefore necessary for the experience or attainment of spiritual liberation and enlightenment. And as bizarre and scary as that idea might be, it also conceals an even stranger paradox, in that an Ego or a sense of self is necessarily an essential component of every kind of attainment or individual experience; in other words, for any experience there must be, by definition, one who experiences.

For a practitioner of yoga, the combination of a disbelief in material reality with faith in a Supreme Being and a radical devaluation of the individual Ego can potentially throw the self off its primary instinctual axis, inverting its natural values by reframing the erasure of the individual self as the highest good. If we make the assumption that subjective consciousness intrinsically requires the existence of a subjective individual self, then the mystical attempt to 'transcend' the self appears to have as its object nothing other than the dissolution of consciousness, if not existence itself. If the mind is viewed as an obstacle and the body as something not to be identified with, there will always be a certain risk of self-damage and the powerful techniques of yoga can actually increase this danger; therefore, in order to practice yoga it is all the more necessary to remain well grounded in material reality and to possess a strong sense of self. Some individuals who discover an obsession with 'spiritual surrender' and the weird pleasures of erasing the Ego in the service of spiritual transcendence might not feel the need to stop until years after the wheels have come completely off their fractured psyches and the grinding of metal on metal becomes impossible to ignore. By contrast, a yoga practitioner who is grounded in realism and possesses a healthy sense of Ego and self-worth can develop in a stronger and more balanced way, developing a stable physical and psychological base from which to explore the depths of the unconscious psyche rather than embarking haphazardly on a madcap one-way journey of self-denial and transcendental escapism.

When 'spiritual' forms or traditions of meditation are discussed, the term 'Ego' is frequently tossed around as if it were a dirty word. This often flies under the radar and seems quite reasonable to most westerners, since humility is generally regarded as a virtue and in English the word Ego often carries connotations of conceit, self-importance, pride, or arrogance. Thus, if a spiritual guru or religious figure of some sort says something along the lines of '*the Ego is the only true obstacle to consciousness and enlightenment*,' it often appears to have a certain ring of commonsense wisdom to it and is rarely objected to.

In the context of Eastern spirituality, however, the Latin word 'Ego' is usually a translation of the Sanskrit word 'ahamkara' or one of its derivatives, which generally denote the totality of the individual mind and the subjective sense of self or differentiation. Note that in this there is no clear demarcation between the mind and the body; as Freud put it 'The Ego is first and foremost a bodily Ego; it is not merely a surface entity, but is itself the projection of a surface.' There is actually some confusion about the use of the word 'Ego' in Freud's work as well, however, which stems from James Strachey's widely used English translation, where Ego was used as a proxy for the German phrase 'das ich,' which literally means 'the I'. Freud himself did not actually use the Latin word 'Ego' in his classic model of the psyche, which in its native German consisted of 'Das Es' ('The It,' translated by Strachey into the Latin term 'Id'), 'Das Ich' ('The I,' translated by Strachey into the Latin term 'Ego') and 'Das Uber-Ich' (literally the 'The Over-I', translated by Strachey into the term 'super Ego'). Twentieth Century English translations of Buddhist and Hindu texts further compounded the confusion by choosing the word Ego, which now has many overarching psychological and Freudian overtones, to translate the Sanskrit word ahamkara. In any case, in Latin the word Ego literally means 'the I,' and so leaving aside the various interpretations of Freud and all of the subtle shades of meaning the word may possess in the English vernacular, as a Latin word it is in the strictest sense a fair translation of the Sanskrit term ahamkara. The point that is often missed, however, is that when the word 'Ego' appears in the context of Eastern spirituality it does not mean 'arrogance' or 'excessive pride'—it always means one thing and one thing only, which is the individual self and the mind.

Since the word ego has multiple meanings in English, its usage is often ambiguous in the context of religion or Eastern spirituality. Spiritual teachers routinely conflate its various meanings, presumably to soften or sugar coat the frightening implications of Ego dissolution in 'mystical transcendence' and lend the process an air of wholesome moral goodness. This can be a genuine source of confusion; consider, for example, what a fairly generic mystical phrase such as 'one must overcome and transcend the ego completely in order to find inner peace and enlightenment' actually means. The mind's relationship with itself is its most intimate core of personal integrity, and if the mind begins regarding its own discrete identity as a major obstacle to 'spiritual enlightenment' or earnestly pursuing the simultaneously grandiose and self-abnegating goal of becoming 'one with everything,' its sense of real personal responsibility and doership starts evaporating almost immediately. A person operating within such a mental framework might refuse to acknowledge 'the I' as ever having done anything, crediting instead the agency of a Supreme Being; ironically, within the confines of such a mystical worldview it is only this I or Ego that is somehow isolated and left out of the otherwise all-encompassing unity of cosmic oneness and therefore targeted for eradication and dissolution.

Of course, an overly acute or overbearing sense of oneself can get in one's way at times; in truth, a big part of Eastern spirituality's appeal for westerners lies in the fact that a smidgen of 'selflessness' can sometimes enhance one's performance in a sporting, business or social context. This is certainly an interesting inner game and a fruitful area of practice: yet even if, in the moment and under pressure, the mind is able to attain a real sense that it is somehow 'doing without doing'—shooting a basketball for instance, or giving a speech or sinking a golf putt—it is nevertheless always the mind of the individual that performs and experiences a particular action, and everyone understands this intuitively on some level. Again, the ability to turn down the volume on one's verbal Ego and to let go of the consciousness of praise and blame under pressure in order to perform at a peak level is a tool of self-mastery that one can reasonably take a certain measure of pride in, an excellent 'fringe benefit' of sorts that comes with the practice of yoga and meditation. However, in a broader psychological context it is obvious that no real self-trust or lasting personal integrity would be possible if one were not able to answer directly to oneself within the privacy of one's own mind, either because that self did not exist or because one was compelled to censor and repress one's thoughts out of the constant fear of an unseen master, which in some sense amounts to the same thing. The fantasy of escaping mystically by 'losing oneself completely' in the omnipresence of a Supreme Being takes this idea even further, incorporating perhaps the unconscious desire of escaping such inner tyranny altogether; carried to its logical conclusion it implies the complete annihilation of the self and a full embrace of the absurd paradox that it is somehow possible to know something by ceasing to know, and to become something by ceasing to exist.

If we think about the number of people who have irreparably harmed themselves through excessive drug abuse we might also wonder how many of them were reassuring themselves all along the way that some 'higher power' beyond their brain and body was always there to protect them from damage, ready to miraculously redeem and repair them from any kind of reckless self-abuse, like an infinitely renewable divine insurance policy. How many of them, we might ask, by implicitly placing their faith in a magical safety net of divine resurrection and immortality have tragically undervalued their physical brains, and in the process gravely underestimated the consequences of their actions; how many have even taken drugs for the express purpose of 'transcending' the mind, imagining that they might thereby reach some alternative state of mystical reality, traveling like abstractions of themselves through cartoonish passageways of hallucination into secret chambers of transcendence. The notion that we exist protected on all sides by a benevolent cosmic intelligence that is always ready to heal and forgive can leave the inexperienced open to underestimating the unforgiving gravity and severity of the world, and to lazily imagining that it is a softer, cozier and more magical place than it actually is. As Hunter S. Thompson put it so coldly in 1971:

'What Leary took down with him was the central illusion of a whole lifestyle that he helped create... a generation of permanent cripples, failed seekers, who never understood the essential old mystic fallacy of the acid culture: the desperate assumption that somebody, or at least some force, is tending the light at the end of the tunnel.' – Hunter S. Thompson, Fear and Loathing in Las Vegas

In its more explicit formulations, an unquestioning belief in the 'transcendent' can form the rational basis of a cult environment, a place where self-negation can be stacked and folded recursively inward upon itself, its fierce internal efforts of mental dissolution made all the more intoxicating by its utter outward insignificance and timid, worthless triviality. Contrary to popular belief, however, becoming truly 'brainwashed' is never easy; the annoying selfhood of the mind stubbornly persists through the most prolonged distortions and austerities, and there is never enough 'spiritual bliss' around to reach a state of lasting amnesia and selflessness. As a consequence, most cultists never make it far beyond the exciting first pretenses of 'spiritual surrender'; once the initial rush wears off, most mind-control environments, no matter how grotesquely conformist or intrusive, eventually reveal themselves to be oppressively boring and mundane. Truly effective 'brainwashing,' therefore, must inevitably be a do-it-yourself project; those who can approach the limit of Ego destruction and self-erasure are always, deep within, collaborators who secretly will it upon themselves, and are continually dissatisfied that their ecstasies of repetition and banality are never quite immersive, disorienting or permanent enough to fully erase the indelible stain of their personal identity.

Of course, some spiritual gurus seem to have understood this dark corner of human nature instinctively, and recognize that the harder something is to believe the more steadfastly those invested in believing it will contort themselves in order to keep believing. And while it might seem paradoxical that selflessness and cognitive dissonance can actually feed upon one another, where there is a will to believe there is also way for the mind to make itself believe, or at least to make itself believe that it believes; on a large enough scale, this kind of thing can also open the door to such distinctly ugly human behaviors as blind, unquestioning obedience and robotic lockstep group cohesion. Again, however, in some sense the mind must always remain aware of itself, and therefore of its inner self-betrayal; this is frequently salved with an incessant stream of inward faithful chatter and rationalization, which conceals beneath its surface an unwillingness to honestly and introspectively level with oneself. Such inner deformations are, to one degree or another, incompatible with yoga and meditation, which have only the self as their object, and for the practice of which the mind requires the full measure of its natural ease and transparency with itself.

In a sense, advanced yoga and meditation happen along the borderlands between the conscious and the unconscious mind, and therefore require a certain ability to 'let go' of oneself. This ability to switch gears from verbal thinking and self-monitoring into a less structured meditative mindset gives one a greater freedom to move up and down the ladder of consciousness, so to speak, while remaining centered within the objective physical self. Consider the simple act of falling asleep: falling asleep is not actually something that can be *done*, per se; from the perspective of the conscious Ego sleep just 'happens' when the mind is able to let go of itself, thus allowing the body to transition naturally into the state of sleep. The conscious mind feels safe in 'letting go' and falling into sleep because it intuitively understands that sleep is temporary and feels confident of being anchored in the body; it knows from experience that it always returns to itself upon awakening, and so the nightly submersion into the oblivion of sleep is easily accepted. Similarly, in meditation and yoga there are moments when one's mental frame might shift, when one might in a sense 'go beyond' oneself in progressing to a new level of concentration or skill; such personal breakthroughs require an ability to 'let go' of oneself while simultaneously remaining grounded in reason and material reality. Therefore yoga, somewhat counter-intuitively, actually requires a strong Ego and a solid sense of self capable of counterbalancing the flexibility and detachment that is so necessary for venturing into the deeper unconscious totality of the psyche.

7

EL SEGUNDO

We sat back on the balcony, staring out over the wide beach below. The toes of her bare feet flexed and spread above the railing, silhouetted by the sharply rendered mouse-grey Moon, which seemed unusually close that night; a cold ocean breeze occasionally whipped up a faint whistling howl along the bike path below.

'Lacan said that a desire to sleep all the time might be an unconscious desire for death,' she said. 'That, if you're always lying around sleeping, in a way you're already dead, or trying to be; you're living in a state which is something like a living death—technically alive, but physically and mentally inert, inactive.'

'Well, that's only if you're not watching TV,' I said. 'But yeah, when I started getting good at yoga I noticed that I enjoyed sleeping a lot more, but it was different than before. It started to have this intense, sweet quality of yogic bliss. My body would feel so good from doing hatha yoga, and then when I went to sleep I was so relaxed, and the more I relaxed the deeper I'd sleep; or in the morning, I'd wake up and be lying there kind of half awake, and I'd just start meditating, and then I'd fall asleep again and I'd still be meditating, relaxing, going even deeper.'

'It's called sloth,' she said, grinning. 'But maybe you're such a degenerate we should think up a cooler name for it.'

'I like sloths,' I said. 'They used to fascinate me, because I could never figure out what they looked like. I was weird like that though. I always thought that the wooly mammoth at the tar pits looked like a chambered nautilus, and I used to have bone chilling nightmares about the Portuguese man of war.'

'I used to dream about this radiant blue butterfly jellyfish,' she said. 'It would sneak in and hover over my dreams, illuminating whatever I was watching; but if I noticed it was there it would instantly wisp away through a secret passageway in the wall.'

'Maybe biology is the true science of dreams,' I said. She sipped her drink and looked at the Moon.

'A long time ago, I stayed with an Indian guru in South America,' she said. 'I loved her dearly; I worshipped her in every way. I'd sit for meditation and stare at her picture for hours.'

'Dharana,' I said. 'Concentration. Dhyana; absorption.'

'Of course. But my point is, eventually I realized I could easily meditate in the same way on anything. I could focus and slow my mind down staring at a picture of *any* object— a cat, a tropical bird, a supermodel on a runway, an athlete, a river, anything.'

'A sloth,' I volunteered.

'Well, I guess that would explain a lot,' she said. She ran her hand back through her hair, then rubbed her nose with the back of her hand. 'But my point is,' she sniffed, 'That when I did this kind of meditation, I felt like I could perceive an object on a deeper level, get a deeper sense of its objective reality. The longer I looked into anything the more real it would become, the more of its details would emerge, the more of itself would be revealed.'

'So you meditate on supermodels?' I asked.

'No,' she said. 'But I am fascinated with beauty. However the point I'm making here is that once I'd freed myself completely from spirituality and superstition, and stopped forcing myself to meditate on transcendent nonsense, it came to me that I could meditate on anything. And if you meditate on anything long enough you'll start to understand it more deeply and intuitively, going beyond any preconceived linguistic definitions or labels.'

'Some people say that the mind begins to take on the color and shape of whatever it focuses on,' I said.

'I think that's closer to a kind of shamanistic concept, which is something completely different,' she said. 'What I'm talking about is just widening and deepening your perception through meditation, allowing yourself to see an object more completely, to grok a sense of its objective reality.'

'Sometimes I wonder where the impulse to meditate even comes from,' I said. 'I'll be meditating, and I'll just wonder, is it me? Am I actually meditating, or is it my unconscious mind? And what's the difference, really? I mean, intellectually, I get that there is no difference, that in a sense I *am* my unconscious mind, and my unconscious mind is me, and consciousness is just the aspect of myself through which I experience self-awareness. But in a way all that is almost like a word game; intuitively, I really only get this sense of organic wholeness within myself when I'm immersed in meditation, and actually centered at the core of my awareness.'

'But...' she said, 'If you have awareness there must be a "you" to have that awareness, to be aware. At some point, it seems as if there must be a level that feels or experiences awareness, but is not itself self-aware. Imagine a large whale: it can see forward, it can swim this way and that; but it can't turn its head to look back and see itself. That part of yourself that you can't "see" introspectively is what is unconscious; but in its own way, maybe it too is conscious. Certainly not in the way we usually think of consciousness, but possibly autonomous and self-aware nonetheless, aware of itself as being distinct from its environment. And in a way it is essentially the actual meat of consciousness—consciousness is merely a more refined and delicate extension of it, whatever "it" might be.'

'So you're saying that if I wasn't an animal, I wouldn't be consciously aware of myself?'

'Well, what do you mean by conscious? If you were a robot or a computer, your self-awareness would lack the peculiar mammalian quality that you've so closely identified with consciousness. Eventually, robots might evolve a kind of sensory self-awareness of their own unconscious metal and silicone corporeality, and this might provide the ground for a form of consciousness. But of course it's likely to be vastly different from the way that you and I think of consciousness.'

8

HATHA YOGA

Hatha yoga, popularly known as the physical or 'stretching' type of yoga, consists of three main parts: pranayama, asana and dhyana. Pranayama is the yogic art of deep breathing and breath control, asana is the practice of yogic poses and body positions, and dhyana is concentration or meditation.

All three of these elements—body position, breathing and meditation—are essential to the art of yoga and are interwoven all through it, overlapping with each other in countless ways. Proficiency in the practice of asana, for instance, requires skill in yogic breathing, which in turn requires proficiency in meditation. In hatha yoga the primary object of concentration is the body; reflective meditation is the key, the wellspring that deepens and animates every aspect of yoga technique and in hatha yoga this begins with concentration on the body. In hatha yoga the mind focuses *completely* on the body: as a practitioner works to find balance and equipoise within each asana the mind is literally meditating upon the physical structure of the body and its connection to consciousness, the flow of its attention concentrated internally onto the muscles, bones, blood vessels and nerves as they pull together and hold the form of each asana. Hatha yoga is explicitly and profoundly physical, and thrives when the mind reaches a point of singular concentration upon the body, in a sense 'seeing' the muscles and other structures of the body from the inside and connecting intimately with the body's native kinesthetic intelligence and low-level consciousness. The hatha yoga technique of concentration upon the body, to the exclusion of everything else, allows the mind to become steady and free of thoughts; it leads eventually to excellent meditation, as the focus of dharana and concentration shifts laterally from the body to the mind, the subject of meditation gradually merging into its object as awareness turns progressively inward upon itself.

The ability to relax the body at will, including the ability to selectively relax specific muscle groups while maintaining isometric muscle tone and balanced extension elsewhere in the body, is an essential skill-set for proficiency in hatha yoga. Along with this, an understanding of the reciprocal relationship between physical tension and emotional stress is key. A physical 'fight-or-flight' response can easily be generated in reaction to imagined or remembered stimuli; another way to say this is that the neocortical regions of the brain are capable of creating thoughts and images that can trick the body into generating real stress responses, which can in turn flood the system with stress hormones like cortisol and adrenaline and create significant muscular tension. Conversely, muscular tension originally created by stress responses to real-world stimuli can be 'stored' in the muscles over time, generating and reinforcing ongoing defensive emotional reactions in the mind that are resistant to purely mental efforts to relax because their emotional underpinnings are in a sense imprinted on the body and held in place physically by unconscious tension. These stored traces of surplus muscular tension can embed emotional pain into 'muscle memories' that point on an unconscious level directly back to stressful or painful events and narratives from one's past; thus, the invisible stimuli for stress and anxiety may remain present in the psyche, just beyond the reach of conscious awareness, held in place by the muscular tension and readiness generated by the body's own self-protective instincts. This self-defeating paradox generally occurs below the threshold of conscious awareness or along the fuzzy borders of the subconscious and can result in people carrying around the physical and emotional tension from long-forgotten events for decades, continuing to respond to them on an emotional level without even being aware of it. Eventually, the body may develop the habit of remaining in a constant state of tension and readiness as a kind of emotional shield or armor, keeping itself continually on-guard even during sleep; in the end, this tension does nothing more than guard against anxiety itself, like a kind of habitual talisman warding off the emotional tension of long forgotten threats, conflicts and dangers, whether real or imagined. This in turn feeds into a kind of recursion, with muscular tension continually reinforcing, recreating and reliving negative emotion, as negative emotion continually and repeatedly invokes muscular tension. The yoga technique for opening and unlocking this kind of deeply ingrained muscular tension is far reaching and profoundly effective; its ability to pull the body out of its shell of self-perpetuating physical tightness and to thus release the mind from ingrained and unnecessary patterns of emotional reaction is one of the major reasons that yoga is such a uniquely effective weapon against stress.

The flipside of using deep relaxation to unlock the body's muscular tension in this way is that it can sometimes cause temporary sensations of anxiety by exposing hidden emotional pain, ripping the protective scabs off difficult mental conflicts and painful memories that may have lain dormant and forgotten for years. It's well known among yoga teachers that students sometimes spontaneously burst into tears during a yoga session, when a tight or guarded area of the body is opened and challenged to release its held tension; the subsequent deep release and the sudden absence of emotionally 'protective' or defensive muscular armor can momentarily leave a student feeling naked and vulnerable, as a hardened piece of their subconscious self-image is suddenly washed away by an onrush of discharged emotional energy. This process of unlocking unconscious muscular tension in the body is at the nexus of what makes yoga so energizing, pleasurable and emotionally liberating, and ultimately so effective at reducing stress. Philosophically, this approach is rooted in the idea that it is a healthy thing for the body and the mind to feel good, to feel uninhibited, free and relaxed, and that the innermost nature of an individual is at its core good, and deserves to thrive, blossom and express itself, rather than be repressed and controlled by external authority.

Hatha yoga can make the body more 'conscious' in the sense that its practice extends the conscious mind deeper into the structures of its muscles, bones and nerves, challenging and cultivating a kind of physical intelligence by forging connections between the higher cognitive centers of the brain and the 'lower' levels of the nervous system, which are sometimes associated with the 'reptilian' component of the Triune Brain model. These lower-level components of the nervous system, such as the basal ganglia and the spinal cord, extend into the structure of the body and control it directly; the higher mental layers that govern abstract thought and consciousness sit atop this sleek primordial machine but at their base are firmly and inextricably rooted in it. A yogi is, in a sense, able to descend the ladder of consciousness within the body, seeking intimate communion with those parts of the unconscious self that directly feel and control the body's extended structure; this is, if you will, a linking or 'yoking' of consciousness *downward* into the body. One of the more esoteric secrets of hatha yoga is that it is rooted in precisely this kind of downward-linkage, from the abstract conscious mind directly down into the vast dark inner jungle of the body, rather than the other way around; in practice, this linking is essential to the body-control, balance and endurance that advanced yogis are so well known for. Obviously, from an atheistic perspective, the traditional yoga concept of linking or 'yoking' the mind 'upward' to a hypothetical Supreme Being is unintelligible; however, in terms of more thoroughly connecting subjective awareness with the physical body, the concept of linking, whether 'upward' or 'downward' (and these distinctions are of course metaphorical), can be understood as an expansion of consciousness, awareness and control further into the physical body.

In hatha yoga one strives to increase subjective body-awareness and control, by narrowing the gap between consciousness and objective physical being. Working with the body using asana and pranayama, the practitioner comes continually closer to consciously perceiving the impulse behind physical movement, the point where mental volition reemerges from the unconscious and is translated into physical action. The slow, repetitive and controlled nature of hatha yoga practice lends itself to continually honing one's inner awareness of how the mind moves the body; in extended physical stillness, the mental impulses behind movement and action come into sharp

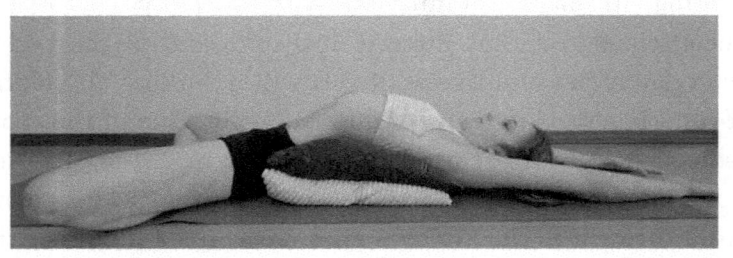

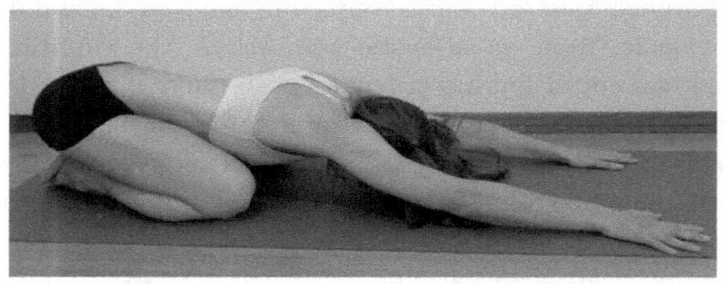

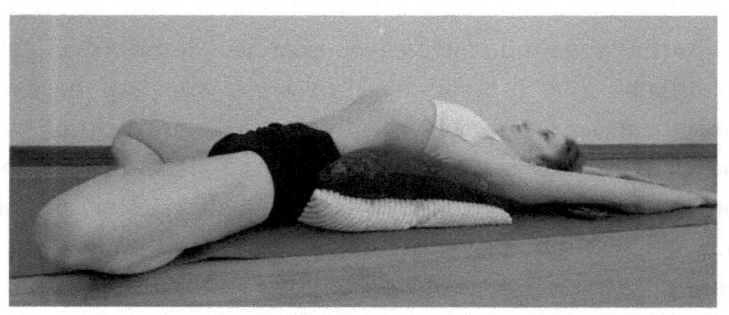

relief. While holding a balanced posture and working with the breath to relax and extend the spine, the mind develops a closer relationship to its ultimately physical nature, as it strives to push the limits of self-awareness and self-control. This naturally leads to a greater consciousness of the biological mechanisms through which the mind's directives and volitions are sent down into the black box of the unconscious mind, to be processed and then to emerge in the body as physical action; the practice of asana can thus be interpreted as a framework for refining and strengthening this kind of highly focused self-awareness and for learning to focus one's mental attention inward toward the connections between consciousness and raw physicality—between the subjective and the objective aspects of the mind and body.

Greater conscious awareness and control of the body makes it progressively easier to root out and defuse muscular tension, allowing one to reach blissfully deep levels of physical and emotional relaxation. Having a thoroughly relaxed body—open, balanced and at ease—removes numerous obstacles to introspection and inward self-absorption, making meditation easier and more enjoyable; in this sense, doing hatha yoga works to develop the body as a steady and balanced physical platform for the practice of meditation, the living touchstone upon which the mind can center itself within the objective physical world.

9

ASANA

Yogic poses, or asanas, include all of the classical body positions of hatha yoga, as well as an array of more recently evolved techniques and positions that are derived from them. Generally speaking, the practice of asana should be understood to include all of the sitting, standing, twisting, bending, arching, inverted and prone body positions used in hatha yoga and meditation as well as the myriad transitions and transformations between them. Literally translated, the Sanskrit word asana means 'base,' 'seat,' or 'foundation,' and this meaning is central to understanding the significance of what an asana truly represents in hatha yoga; in an esoteric sense, each yogic pose constitutes, in its own way, a solid 'seat' and foundation for consciousness. When performed correctly, each asana contains at its core a point of balance and singular stillness; this is the seat of the asana, the motionless hub at the center of the body's extension. No matter how complex, inverted or contorted an asana might appear outwardly, at its center there is always a point of balance and repose pointing solidly North and South—a mental connection to the body's physical center of balance, its unmoving zero gravity core in any particular position. This is one of the subtle secrets of advanced hatha yoga; when the mind can focus in this way during yoga practice every asana deepens and comes to life, generating absorption, energy, bliss and concentration.

A strong 'base' is essential to the practice of asana; like the base of a statue, an intuitive understanding of how to orient and root oneself perpendicular to the pull of gravity makes every position more stable, relaxed and grounded. This kind of solid foundation allows for controlled extension of the spine, which is one of the primary goals of modern hatha yoga; the body works actively within a pose, isometrically extending itself against the pull of gravity. In standing poses, the lower body forms a solid base for the trunk and upper body, the feet pushing downward into the floor, the legs and butt firm and stable, and the inner thighs flexing upward into the crotch as the spine lifts out of the pelvis and extends through the top of the head toward the sky. In inverted poses like headstand the lower body works in the opposite direction, extending itself upward toward the ceiling through the soles of the feet as the neck and shoulders stabilize the posture below and the head and forearms push downward into the ground. In both standing and inverted postures the legs are held firm and the core is held tensed and active; the torso lengthens, isometrically extending the spine as if it were being pulled from both ends. A similar dynamic is also at work in seated and reclining asanas, and requires finding an internal point of equilibrium between the body and the pull of gravity in order to properly align the pelvis and lengthen the spine upward.

Theoretically, it should be possible to master the entire art of hatha yoga by perfecting a single asana, since all of the attributes required for mastery are potentially contained in each and every asana. The classic example for illustrating this principle is Tadasana, or the Mountain Pose. Tadasana is the simplest and most fundamental of all the asanas and yet, in a certain sense, every asana is contained in Tadasana; it might even be possible to say that every asana *is* Tadasana. On its surface, Tadasana appears as seemingly nothing more than an erect standing posture, straight with the arms held at the sides, the neck elongated, and the head facing forward. Given the simplicity of the position, which is obviously not unique to yoga, it might well be asked what can possibly be meant by saying that every yoga asana is Tadasana? And what does this tell us about the nature of yoga?

The first thing to understand is that, despite its outward appearance, Tadasana is actually quite complex, and involves far more than merely standing at attention. To begin with, in the correct practice of Tadasana the lower body is always firm and engaged, and alive; the legs lengthen from the inner groin downward all the way through the inner ankles, as the feet press actively into the floor, and the kneecaps lift upward as the quadriceps hold the legs straight. The weight of the body is balanced evenly across all four corners of both feet, which press into the ground and widen, the toes spreading and feeling the floor. Both femurs rotate inwardly, isometrically counterbalanced by the forward push of the tailbone; this inward rotation of the femurs tends to make the butt stick out by pushing the tailbone backward, while the opposite action of pulling the tailbone forward and under tends to open the hips and rotate the femurs outward. When these opposing actions are pitted against each other this is what is called 'actively working' within the pose: the body is held firm and straight in Tadasana as the opposing muscle groups push evenly against one another in tandem; the resulting front to back squeeze brings the pelvis into alignment and lengthens the torso as it extends upward from the lower body.

The core is also active and engaged in the proper performance of Tadasana; the navel pulls back toward the front of the spine, the pelvic floor lifts, and the abdominal and lower back muscles are activated and firm. At the same time, the spine extends and lifts out of the pelvis, lengthening upward through the top of the head. The complex sheaths of muscle wrapped around the spine flex and pull in four directions, creating space between each vertebra, dynamically supporting and elongating it from the sacrum to the base of the skull. The upper back widens, and the shoulder blades pull away from each other, as the chest spreads open and the deltoids are pulled back slightly; this simultaneous pushing and pulling action flattens the body laterally, and holds the shoulders square and aligned with the hips. The arms reach downward, lengthening along the side of the body through the fingertips, and the neck is held long, the ears lifting upward away from the shoulders. The eyes are soft and relaxed, yet focused and aware; the breathing is active and diaphragmatic, and the mind is composed into focused stillness at the body's center of gravity.

Here is a picture of Tadasana, with graphics added to illustrate some of the crosscurrents of muscular counter-tension that are involved in the position, especially the interaction between the inward rotation of the femurs and the forward push of the sacral triangle, and between the upward extension of the spine and the downward press of the lower body and feet into the floor. The way the body interacts with itself to generate a kind of four-way isometric traction within Tadasana brings into focus two of the fundamental objectives of hatha yoga practice in general: proper alignment of the hips and pelvis, and extension of the spine. These objectives are of central relevance in the practice of virtually every other asana in hatha yoga.

The principles of yogic technique contained in Tadasana are fundamental to every position in hatha yoga, including headstands and shoulder stands, twisting poses, seated and prone positions, standing poses, forward stretches and backbends. There is, of course, a vast array of distinctions and technical variations among the various asanas of hatha yoga, and this seemingly inexhaustible complexity is one of the reasons that hatha yoga is such a deep art. It is a fact, however, that the technical attributes on display in Tadasana—extension and lengthening of the spine, alignment of the hips and pelvis, firmness of the lower body, a flexed and activated core, the inner push and pull of isometric counter-tension, firm and steady balance, concentrated mental focus, diaphragmatic breathing and breath control, and intense body-awareness and kinesthetic introspection—are all in one way or another integral to every other asana in hatha yoga. This peculiar blend of qualities and facets belongs uniquely to yoga; hatha yoga's use of muscular counter-tension to generate traction for extending the spine and spreading the shoulders and hips, for example, or its outward aspect of solid stillness, which mirrors its intense reflective internal focus, mark it as significantly different from arts such as gymnastics or dance. Some non-yogis are highly flexible, and can easily perform impressive external stretches and contortions, but only in a way that is limp and unfocused, and lacks the inner dimensions and the solid, balanced

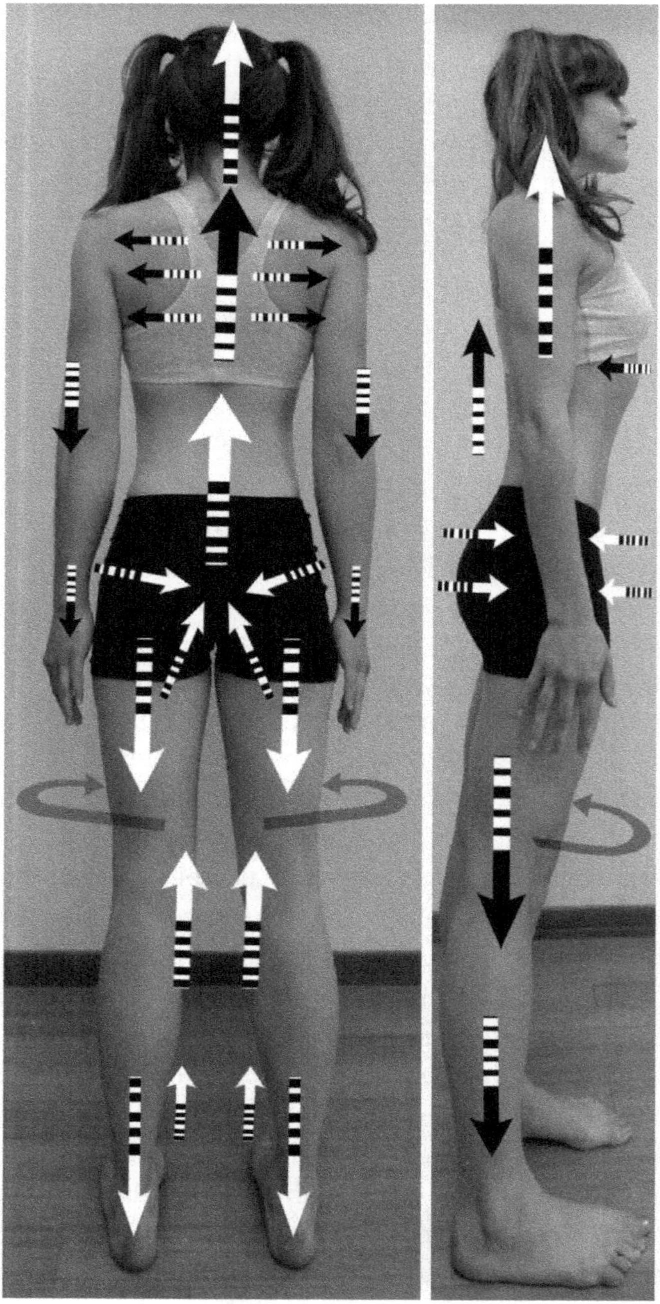

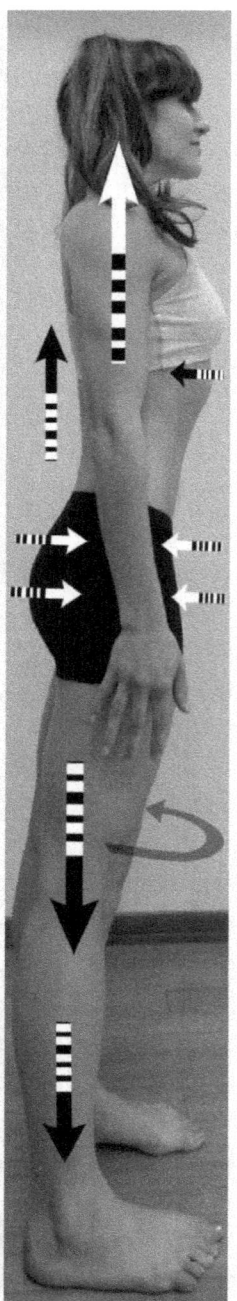

base so characteristic of yoga. Every hatha yoga asana shares some of the same yoga DNA, and therefore mastering any one particular asana will necessarily cultivate general attributes that are applicable to every other asana as well. In this sense, each asana or technique is always an entry point into the full art of yoga, a doorway that can open up and reveal its underlying complexity when approached with determined and consistent effort. This is, to be sure, a somewhat advanced way of thinking about asana practice; such an approach, however, can also immediately deepen and energize practice for students at any level, and can allow beginners who may only know one or two techniques to begin to get a taste of the deeper 'flavor' of real yoga.

The following pictures show some well-known yoga positions and attempt to illustrate some of the dynamics of muscular push and pull or counter-tension they contain. Note that these illustrations are not accompanied by any descriptions or instructions, and the positions are not named, either in English or in Sanskrit; this is by design, in keeping with this chapter's emphasis on the general principles and attributes of hatha yoga as opposed to its technical minutiae. While examining these pictures, think about the concept of holding each pose while actively working inside it to extend and adjust the body in concert with yogic breathing; in this kind of practice, one's mental concentration should be completely focused on the body, working from the inside of its muscles, nerves and bones, and fixating from within on the center of gravity at its centermost core, the x-axis that bisects the body down the middle into a left and a right hemisphere.

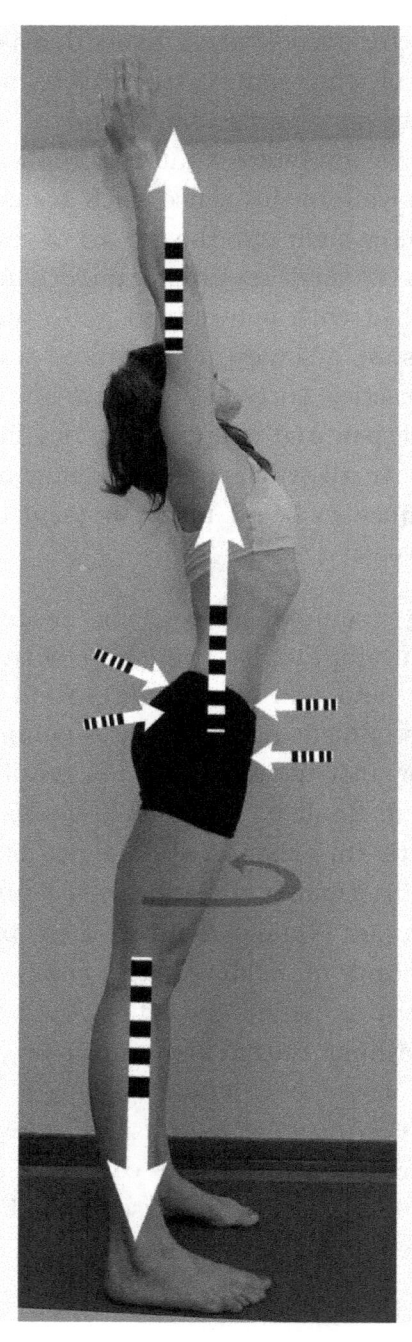

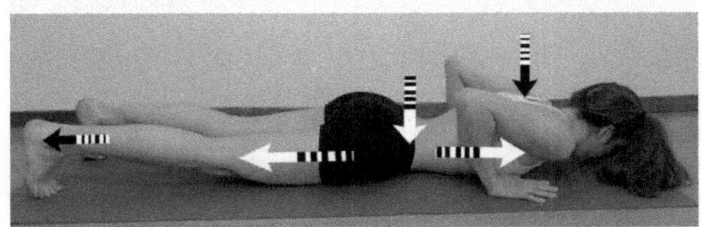
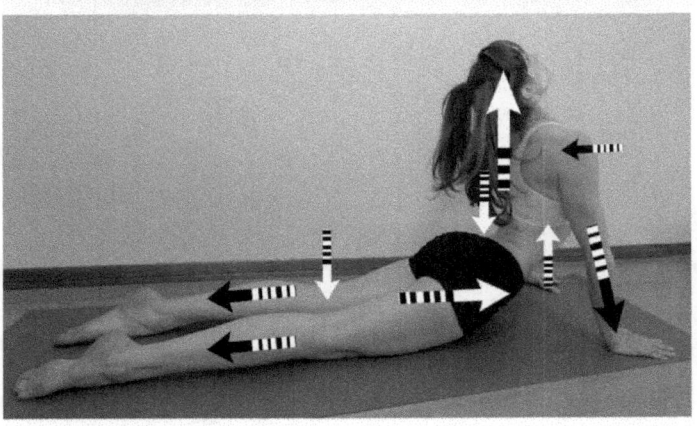

10

THE CORE

The core is the muscular center-mass of the body, consisting of the diaphragm, the abdominal muscles, the lower back, the pelvic floor, and all of their various synergistic interconnections. The core can be visualized as a cylinder: the diaphragm is the top of this cylinder, the abdominal and lower back muscles are its rounded sides, and the pelvic floor is its bottom. The muscles of the core connect and interact with each other in many complex ways; this simplified conceptualization, however, of the core as a virtual cylinder of muscle extending from the diaphragm to the pelvic floor, is an excellent representation of its overall structure and synergy. Together, the muscles of the core form the center of the body's functional strength and support, and are the key component for good posture, balance, agility, coordination, physical fitness and sexual attractiveness.

The top of the cylinder, the diaphragm, is a layer of muscle separating the upper and lower torso, connecting to the rib cage and forming a seal separating the lungs and the heart from the viscera and abdominal organs below. During inhalation, the diaphragm pulls downward, becoming concave; this downward pull of the diaphragm opens the rib cage and draws air into the lungs. Exhalation is the opposite of inhalation; during exhalation, the diaphragm pushes upward and becomes convex, pulling the ribs together and squeezing air from the lungs. That the diaphragm actually pulls *downward* during inhalation, and pushes *upward* during exhalation may seem at first to be counterintuitive because the chest often seems to 'rise' with the inhalation and to 'fall' with the exhalation. However, that rising and falling of the chest is really more like an expansion and contraction; the chest and rib cage swell with air and expand on the inhale, then flatten and contract as air is pushed out on the exhale. Although the rib cage expands and contracts during breathing, the action of the diaphragm is always up and down; again, visualize the diaphragm as the top of a cylinder, drawing downward into a concave shape during inhalation, and rounding upward into a convex shape during exhalation.

The idea of yogic core breathing is to actively engage the diaphragm, exaggerating the expansion and contraction of the ribcage; with each breath, the ribs should be felt to expand outward toward the front, side and back during inhalation, filling the lungs with air, and to contract inward firmly during exhalation, pushing the air out. This kind of active diaphragmatic breathing adds energy to the practice of yoga, filling the lungs completely, activating and energizing the muscles of the core, oxygenating the body and increasing extension of the spine.

The bottom of the core cylinder is the pelvic floor; it consists of a web of muscles that intertwine under and through the pelvis, including the Pubococcygeus, the Iliopsoas and the Piriformis. The Pubococcygeus, or PC, muscle extends from the pubis to the tailbone; it is closely linked to the genitals, and is one of the muscles that contract involuntarily in rhythmic spasms during sexual orgasm. Improving the strength of the PC muscle strengthens the entire excretory and reproductive systems. In the male, it increases control of ejaculation, and in the female, it improves vaginal tone and muscle control; in both sexes, it increases the potential for multiple orgasms. A strong PC muscle is also highly beneficial for the male prostate gland, as it improves circulation and muscle tone in the surrounding tissue, thus nourishing the area with oxygen and fresh blood and clearing out accumulated toxins. The ability to actively flex and engage—or relax—the muscles of the pelvic floor at will during yoga gives the practitioner an extra measure of control and dominion over this area that might otherwise be, by default, a largely unconscious and peculiarly vulnerable soft underbelly of both the body and the psyche. In classical yoga, the practice of mentally focusing on the perineum and contracting it is known as Mula bandha, or the root lock; this technique is highly significant in meditation and breath control. Mula bandha is often confused with aswini mudra, also known as the 'horse' mudra, which consists of the contraction and 'lifting' of the anus or the anal mouth. The difference between these two techniques is somewhat subtle, as in practice they tend to overlap considerably; in any event, both have the effect of 'grounding' and centering awareness within the physical body, and creating a greater sense of ownership and connection from the higher cognitive faculties down to the geographically distant but vitally essential Southern outposts of the nervous system in the regions of the anus and perineum.

When engaging and flexing the muscles of the pelvic floor during yoga practice, visualize pulling them together and inward, as if flexing and tightening the bottom of the core cylinder, lifting it upward into a more convex shape. Also, keep in mind that one must be able to relax the deep muscles of the pelvic floor as well, some of which are difficult to control consciously; learning to flex and activate the pelvic floor, however, makes the inverse task of learning to relax those muscles that much easier. Since the pelvic floor is the bottom of the core, mastery of these muscles will allow you to better control and engage the entire core, and thus the entire body, during yoga practice; a core cylinder with a strong and flexible bottom is a tremendous asset in all phases of hatha yoga practice.

During yoga practice the muscles of the abdomen and the lower back, the 'sides' of the core cylinder, are activated by a moderate isometric squeezing and lifting action, which pulls the lower torso together and generates firm muscle tone and support. The abdominal and lower back muscles interact with the process of deep core breathing with a kind of inside-out pulling and pushing action, squeezing and contracting the core while lifting and extending it. Imagine the core cylinder during diaphragmatic breathing: on inhalation, the top of the cylinder squeezes downward as the diaphragm becomes concave, and on exhalation the process is reversed, as the top of the cylinder becomes convex. In both instances, the muscles of the abdomen and the lower back can either squeeze inward isometrically or lift and lengthen the torso, or both. The net effect is that the core cylinder is actively and consciously flexing and adjusting in relation to the expansion and contraction of the breath on a moment to moment basis, allowing for precise balance and control in both static and moving positions. This combination of deep breathing with core muscle flexion creates an active and 'alive' core, energizing and oxygenating the entire lower torso, and giving rise to better overall muscle tone, feel, balance and control.

We are now going to look at several techniques for 'finding' and activating the core. During yoga practice, there should be continual work on awareness and control of the core muscle groups; note that this also includes cultivating the ability to relax the muscles of the core, as well as the ability to selectively relax *some* of the muscles, while actively flexing and tightening others. This requires considerable practice and experimentation; the following techniques illustrate some of the fundamentals of working with the core, but it should be remembered that they are only starting points.

1. Lie down flat on your back with the soles of your feet on the ground and your knees bent. Relax your abdominal muscles completely. Take a deep breath, and as you exhale, allow your abdomen to flatten and 'suck' gently inward; as you do this, pull your belly button downward through your body toward the spine, and moderately flex the abdominals. You should feel a certain 'pull' or engagement of the lower abdominal muscles; try to hold onto this inward flex for a moment and take a few breaths without letting it go. Now, relax the abdomen, allowing it to become supple and soft, and breathe normally.

2. Stand with your hands on your hips. Take a deep breath, and as you exhale, imagine that you are cinching a belt tightly around your waist, contracting and pulling in the muscles of your abdomen and lower back as you do so, and simultaneously lengthening your torso upward slightly. Continue to breathe actively with your diaphragm, opening your rib cage while inhaling. Now contract the muscles of the PC and the pelvic floor, pulling them upward. Continue breathing, and try to feel the core cylinder expanding and

contracting in three dimensions: upward and downward, front to back, and left to right.

3. Stand up, bending at the knees and leaning forward, placing your hands on your thighs. Lengthen your spine forward, lifting your head slightly. Take a deep breath; as you exhale, pull your navel in toward your spine, hollowing your abdominal cavity into a concave shape. Allow your exhalation to create a kind of vacuum, pulling your navel closer in to the spine; at the same time, moderately flex your abdominal and oblique muscles, as well as the muscles of the lower back. Flex and lift the muscles of the pelvic floor, and breathe actively with the diaphragm. Work between the expansion and contraction of the rib cage, and the hollowing and flex of the abdominal muscles. A few breaths while holding the flex is sufficient for a single repetition; be careful that you don't overdo it with this technique. After each repetition, stand up straight and take a few normal breaths. To intensify the technique, let your head fall forward and arch your back upward; this generally increases the hollowness of the abdomen and the inward 'vacuum' or pull of the navel toward the spine. The trick to this technique is not to merely flex or squeeze the abdominal muscles, but to let them grip onto and engage with the inward pull that the position generates, and then to increase the flex without losing that engagement.

There does exist a certain element of confusion about how what we are describing as 'the core' relates to the area of the body, significant in Taoism, Zen and various of the Asian martial arts, which is called the 'dantian' in Chinese, or the 'tanden' or 'hara' in Japanese. Martial arts such as Karate, Kung-Fu, Jiu-Jitsu, and Qigong, as well as some flavors of Zen meditation, teach that this spot is the center of the body's 'ki' or 'chi,' something generally described as a human distillation of organic life-force, or in more metaphysical terms as a form of 'cosmic' energy that can be stored and channeled within the body with practice. While employing the idea of chi-energy as a metaphor for the circulation of blood, oxygen and nerve impulses throughout the body or as an analogue for mental willpower is not altogether unreasonable, we must also be absolutely clear that this is not in any way a supernatural or mystical concept; we should be similarly realistic regarding the fact that there can in actuality be no precise location for the dantian spot within the human body, since it does not objectively correspond to any of the body's anatomical structures.

Traditionally, the approximate location of the dantian or tanden within the body is in the lower frontal quadrant of the 'core cylinder' as we have described it, approximately three finger-widths below the belly button, and about half that distance to the body's center; this a sensitive area of the body, rich in nerves and blood vessels, which closely approximates an individual's standing center of gravity. The Zen practice of centering the mind here has a lot of merit, as this area is exquisitely corporeal and is in a sense the center of the body's physicality; steadfastly focusing the mind in this spot is an excellent way to quiet one's thoughts inside of meditation and to center oneself in the experience of physical being. The martial arts practice of generating power and torque by tensing this spot when springing into action is also very effective and, combined with Zen centering techniques, can be used to generate a formidable unity of will, intention, balance and physical force. In the practice of yoga, 'gripping' and tightening from this area can allow one to hold oneself

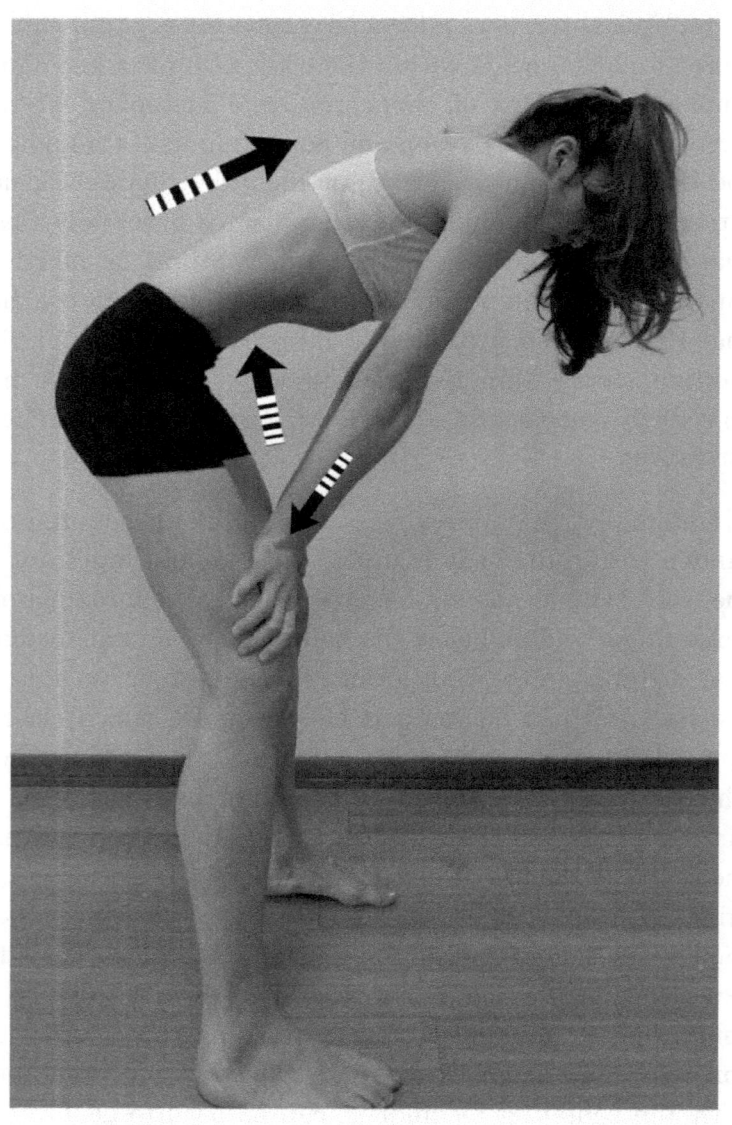

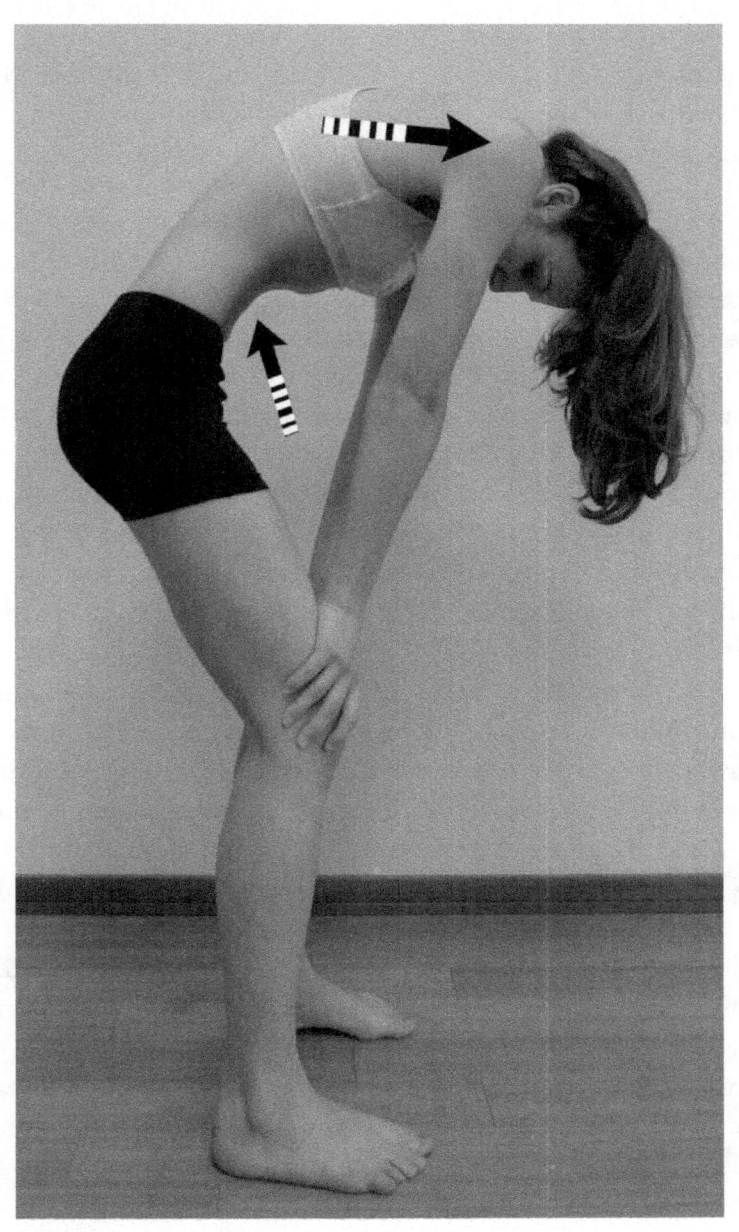

steadily balanced in difficult positions; conversely, releasing all tension from this area and relaxing it completely can be deeply soothing to the entire body, allowing the abdomen to become supple, and respiration to flow smoothly and easily.

It should be noted that this kind of 'letting go' of and relaxing the core below the navel using the breath is fully compatible with the technique for performing Tadasana detailed in the previous chapter; this kind of adjustment, in fact, is inherent in the position, and naturally begins to emerge as one's understanding of the position develops. In this, there is a subtle contradiction that the advanced practitioner will need to puzzle out on a physical level, which involves finding the balance between tension and relaxation in the body, especially in the abdominal core. Lifting and firming the core in Tadasana while simultaneously relaxing the center of the body below the navel is a matter of balancing and blending two seemingly contradictory actions: tightening and squeezing the abs inward, while at the same time allowing the deep lower belly and upper perineal muscles to remain supple and relaxed. The overall centrality of the 'dantian' area, and the delicate control required to relax it and breathe smoothly while simultaneously flexing and tightening the rest of the abdominal core, makes it an excellent spot to focus the mind during asana, meditation and deep breathing practice. Simply put, excellent awareness and control of this area of the body is an absolutely key factor for real skill in hatha yoga. Relaxing and 'opening' this area can also be significant psychologically, as its close proximity to the genitals and the lower viscera make it a vital nexus of instincts and emotions; excessive physical tension here can constrict the entire body, thereby also constricting one's personality and emotional spectrum significantly. An exaggerated example of this would be the stereotypical posture of insecurity, fear or emotional distress, which often appears as being bent forward at the waist, hunched over with the arms crossed protectively in front. The connection and proximity of this area of the body to powerful feelings and emotions, both positive and negative, should not be underestimated; it should be kept in mind that in using yoga to work with the lower core, we are inevitably unlocking deep stores of physical tension from a profoundly vulnerable area of the body, and thus it should not be a surprise if unpleasant emotions are occasionally experienced during practice.

Again, since the dantian does not exist as a discrete anatomical structure, and is obviously not some kind of supernatural energy field within the body, it can best be described as an area of the body that, because of its centrality, is kinesthetically sensitive and therefore in a sense 'intelligent,' in the sense that it is intimately linked to the body-awareness of the unconscious mind. Although essentially metaphorical, the traditional dantian concept is actually quite useful as it is integral to deep breathing and maps well to the body's center of gravity, as well as pointing toward the concept of the body's native kinesthetic intelligence; some have described this area of the body as a kind of 'second brain' within the abdomen, and the ability to let go of tension there is integral to the process of deep relaxation. Yogis, dancers, martial artists and athletes that possess core-awareness are able to move 'from their center' and to control their bodies with fluid balance and agility. This neuromuscular crossroads between the navel and the pubis seems to possess a kind of kinesthetic compass, if you will, a lower body 'inner ear', that allows for an infinity of intricate and delicate balance shifts and transitions even in the trickiest and most difficult spots. The meditative application of this ability lies in being able to focus the mind on the feeling or sense of gravity and balance as it is felt in the center of the body below the navel, often experienced as a subtle tingle of weightlessness or intuition, decipherable as left, right, up, down, front or back. For instance, whether one is leaning forward or backward, being pushed or pulled, or finds oneself upside down, running, jumping or falling, if the mind is sufficiently adept at perceiving the yaw, pitch and roll of the core's inner gyroscope, it will be able to continually readjust and rebalance the body's position and muscular tension, thus making the entire body more responsive and thus in a sense more conscious. This single complex attribute can at times allow one to react from one's physical and emotional 'center' with catlike agility, tapping into the body's native physical intelligence. In the practice of hatha yoga, such core-awareness is a tremendous asset, allowing one to find balance, control and power in any position or transition and enhancing the sense of connection or 'oneness' with the objective physical body.

11

PRANAYAMA

'The walls of the tunnel were undulating, closing in on the dodecahedron, squeezing it forward. A nice rhythm was being established. Every time the dodec would slow almost to a halt, it was given another squeeze by the walls.' – Carl Sagan, Contact

Pranayama is the ancient yogic art of breath control. Although frequently misunderstood, it is nonetheless an amazingly sophisticated and effective method of changing and interacting with the body's physiological rhythms and responses in order to relax, soothe, energize and stimulate the central nervous system. Breath control gives the yoga practitioner a powerful internal handle on the body for adjusting and attenuating its levels of physical and emotional arousal and for transitioning smoothly into relaxed and meditative states of mind. Yogic deep breathing and breath control is integral to the practice of meditation, not only as a powerful tool of physical relaxation, but also as a profound focal point for concentrated introspection; this stems from the fact that respiration is the most primary and fundamental of biological processes, and is therefore functionally rooted in the deepest unconscious and autonomic regions of the psyche. Controlling and closely observing one's breathing during meditation can bring one into direct contact with the innate impulse and rhythm of respiration, something that is largely invisible to the conscious mind and yet is present at every moment of life; such meditation, therefore, can potentially expand self-awareness and self-control in a uniquely powerful and tangible way.

For the sake of realism, it is necessary to dispense with any mystical or supernatural concepts of yogic breath control from the outset. It is, for instance, essential to discard the metaphysical notion of a cosmic life-energy or 'prana' filling the air, which can be accumulated within the body through yogic breath control. Since it is true that every creature on Earth needs to breathe air in order to live, the metaphor of air as a universal life force is a very good one; however from a modern rational perspective it is very well understood that the Earth's atmosphere consists of physical gases—oxygen, nitrogen, carbon dioxide and so forth—and that respiration is essentially a process of gas exchange between living bodies and the external world; there is therefore no reason to strain one's imagination or credulity in order to squeeze the ancient concept of prana into a modern worldview. By explicitly discarding any mystical notions about prana or pranayama we preemptively clear away a lot of confusing philosophical underbrush and leave ourselves a clear path for describing yogic breath control more precisely, in terms of its physiological, emotional and psychological effects. While it certainly must be acknowledged that the breath control techniques of classical yoga are extremely sophisticated and represent literally thousands of years of insight and evolution, in approaching them from a modern scientific perspective it is important that we are clear about precisely what yogic breathing is, and what it is not; we otherwise risk misunderstanding these techniques by conflating them with mysticism, and thus eventually falling into the dead-end quicksand of superstition and magical thinking.

Visualizing the flow of nerve energy, oxygen and blood within one's body can be a potent and useful technique for integrating yogic breath control with meditation; this type of visualization, however, should always strive to conform to a realistic image of one's personal anatomy, and should not get bogged down in fanciful or imaginary conceptions of subtle or mystical 'energy anatomy.' In the practice of yoga and yogic breath control, it is what we could call 'human energy,' and human energy alone, that we are dealing with; losing sight of this, and trying to superimpose upon oneself a preconceived mystical conception of reality, has an immediate cost in terms of clarity and accurate self-perception. In yoga meditation it is important that one's mind remains open, clear and receptive to perceiving the permutations and presence of consciousness even if it presents itself in new and unexpected ways. The real breakthroughs and insights achieved in meditation are invariably surprising and fresh; considered logically, how could such spontaneous perceptions or flashes of enlightenment possibly conform to any trite laundry list of readymade spiritual expectations or experiences that anybody could mimic or learn from a book? In real meditation the willingness to truly listen, unconditionally, to what the body and the mind are saying to you is the most vital of attributes; even while applying oneself to yogic technique with the utmost diligence and effort it is vital to remain open to the direct perception of one's own body and mind in the present moment, to be willing to bend and flow with new and spontaneous insights and intuitions as they occur rather than blindly conforming oneself to any kind of rigidly delineated structure.

In general terms, there are three broad classifications of yogic breathing or pranayama: deep breathing, breath retention (kumbhaka), and rapid forceful breathing (bhastrika). Together, these three fundamental yogic breathing techniques, all of them fairly simple to learn, are sufficient for the successful practice of hatha yoga and meditation, and offer unlimited scope for self-development and training. Note that technical variations such as alternate-nostril breathing can generally be combined with any of the fundamental breath control techniques, and thus should be regarded as variations and not as separate categories of pranayama. Alternate-nostril breathing, sometimes referred to Anuloma pranayama, consists of covering or blocking one nostril with a thumb or forefinger while breathing in or out through the other nostril. The nostril being covered is either alternated after a specific amount of time or a specific number of breaths, or is alternated after each inhalation and each exhalation, so that one is breathing in through the left nostril and out through the right nostril, or vice versa. This technique is certainly not essential for the practice of yogic breathing and should be regarded merely as an interesting variation that some practitioners find useful and energizing in combination with other breathing techniques; it is described here merely in the interest of demystifying a somewhat shadowy and arcane corner of the art. I've encountered various explanations of how alternate-nostril breathing may possibly interact with the body's circadian rhythms, or with the balance between the sympathetic and the parasympathetic nervous systems; as far as I know, however, such causal relationships have never been definitively described or quantified by empirical science or research. It is therefore recommended that, rather than accepting on faith any assumptions about the value or purpose of such techniques, each individual should simply trust their own judgment and intuition about them.

The essential take-away from this section should be that the best way to improve one's skill in pranayama does not lie in technical intricacies or formulas but rather in the cultivation of individual attributes such as body-control and self-awareness, which must be cultivated through introspective practice over time. The idea that a special technique will somehow hold the key to progress can be dangerous; it is always crucial to listen what your body is telling you, and to remain calibrated and 'in tune' with those primary intuitions. This becomes easier through meditation, and is a key component of progress: trusting oneself, and gaining ownership of techniques by puzzling through them and experiencing them deeply and subjectively. Breathing or respiration is fundamental to the process of life, and every individual yoga practitioner that works with pranayama should be acutely aware of this simple fact. Yogic breath control should be approached carefully, with sensitivity and compassion toward one's own body and with an eye not only to what is effective but also to what feels right, personally and subjectively, as opposed to mechanically implementing a series of techniques gotten from a book as if one were applying a whip to a two-dimensional rented mule.

Deep breathing

Yogic deep breathing can be described as a deepening and lengthening of the inhalation and the exhalation that actively involves the abdominal core. The belly is relaxed during inhalation and then tensed slightly, the navel pulling inward, during exhalation. The diaphragm pulls downward expanding the ribs outward during inhalation, filling the lungs completely in every direction; during exhalation, the diaphragm lifts upward and the rib cage squeezes firmly inward, emptying the lungs completely while the spine simultaneously lengthens and relaxes. By actively controlling and lengthening one's breathing in this way its rhythm is slowed down, even as oxygenation is increased, an energizing and relaxing cocktail that begins to soothe the body with micro-cascades of pleasant endorphins almost immediately. Deepening the breath by consciously involving the diaphragm and expanding the rib cage in order to fill the lungs completely, especially the backs of the lungs, increases oxygen flow to the entire body, creating a feeling of lightness and relaxed inner space, an expansiveness that enables one to slow down the rhythm of the breath even further.

This kind of deep breathing is commonly combined with progressive relaxation, and is often practiced in a passive reclining position, either lying flat or supported by a couch or cushions. One of the obstacles here is that the deep breathing and resultant oxygenation can sometimes make one feel mentally active, energized and even restless; there are various reasons for this, but the point here is that in practical terms there is no reason to subject oneself to dry hollow boredom in order to do deep yoga breathing—it's perfectly acceptable to watch TV or listen to music while practicing. Of course, this kind of deep breathing is also often combined with asana practice, in which case it begins to shade over into its more active forms; in the passive form of the practice, however, the emphasis should be the gradual release of tension from the body. A common visualization for this is to imagine breathing 'into' the body, and then exhaling tension 'out' of the body; this can be accentuated by lightly tensing one's muscles during inhalation, and then releasing that tension during exhalation while continuing the deep core breathing uninterrupted. When delved into after one is already focused and absorbed in meditation, this kind of breathing can be an engine of pure physical and mental bliss, smoothing the thoughts from one's forehead and gently pulling the body through level after level of deep relaxation, while feeding a surplus of fresh oxygen to its muscles, nerves and vital organs.

Kumbhaka

What we will here refer to as kumbhaka, or yogic breath retention, can be regarded as a natural progression from deep core breathing, from slowing and extending the breath to holding it and pausing it completely, in order to lengthen the gap between each exhalation and inhalation. This momentary pause in the action of breathing, whether one is holding the breath 'in,' after an inhalation, or 'out,' with the lungs empty after exhalation, quickly focuses the mind and has an energizing effect on the body, especially the core; it is also known to increase cerebral blood flow, as a reflexive response to an increase of CO_2 in the blood. The basic technique of breath retention or kumbhaka is simple: hold the breath for a few seconds, either *in* after inhaling, or *out* after exhaling. This technique can easily be combined and interspersed with deep breathing and relaxation, and at times occurs spontaneously during meditation; it can also be worked into even the most rigorous forms of asana practice. Breath retention should, of course, only be performed under safe conditions (not, for example, while driving a car), and only for brief durations or intervals. Obviously, if you have never used this technique before, or have any doubts regarding its suitability for your current level of physical fitness, you should first consult with a physician or with a qualified yoga instructor.

Classically, yogic breath retention is combined with Mula bandha, Jalandhara bandha and Uddihyana bandha: Mula bandha is the 'root lock,' performed by contracting the anus and the perineum; Jalandhara bandha is the 'throat lock,' performed by releasing the head forward and placing the chin on the chest; Uddihyana bandha is performed by sucking the belly inward and upward during exhalation, creating a kind of abdominal 'vacuum.' Together, these three 'bandhas' combine with the kumbhaka breath retention technique to form one of the classic combinations of hatha yoga. A simple way to implement this technique is to contract the anus and perineum up into the 'root lock' during inhalation, and then hold the breath in; during the subsequent exhalation, the abdomen is pulled inward and upward with a vacuum-like action, the diaphragm squeezing up under the ribcage and emptying the lungs completely. Then, as the lungs are held empty for a moment, the head is tilted forward and the chin placed onto the chest in Jalandhara bandha; an additional adjustment here is to sit up straighter, lengthening the spine and increasing the vacuum-like inward pull of the abdominal muscles. The abdomen is then relaxed as the next inhalation begins, leading either directly into another repetition of pranayama, or back into normal breathing; there is no fixed rule as to the number of repetitions or their duration.

This is a powerful technique. New practitioners are occasionally startled by the sudden sensation of mental stillness that can descend, unannounced, during the elongated space after an exhalation and before the next inhalation; with patient practice, one can use this technique to both soothe and center the body during deep meditation, and to pull oneself deeper into physical and mental relaxation. Keep in mind that the Mula, Uddihyana and Jalandhara bandhas can all be used individually or in various combinations, with or without breath retention, according to one's personal tastes and inclinations. This requires practice and experimentation, and it can of course be helpful to get firsthand instruction from a local yoga instructor, or to watch instructional videos in order to get a clearer idea of how these techniques are used. The main point to remember is that, correctly practiced, these techniques should be easy, not strenuous; they should be conducive to relaxation and to the release of physical and mental tension and progress toward coolheaded and introspective meditation.

A key here is that there is a slight tensing or contraction in the smooth muscle of the circulatory system when the breath is held in after an inhalation, which is subsequently released upon exhalation; an analogy for this might be the way the breath is often held in when straining to lift or move something heavy, and is afterward released with a sigh of relief. This effect can be used to one's advantage: it can be accentuated by a slight deliberate tensing of a targeted body area as the breath is held in, followed by the explicit release of that tension upon exhalation. This could be applicable to, for instance, the sore congested area between two vertebrae, or the tense epicenter of a stress headache in the back of one's head. The action of the breath at the level of the epithelium and the smooth muscle of the circulatory system is combined with focused kinesthetic awareness, in order to soothe and unlock tension in tight corners of the body that may be out of reach of the skeletal muscles, in order to free up the unhindered flow of circulation. Working with yogic deep breathing and breath retention in this way is an extremely effective tool for progressing into deeper states of relaxation, as inevitably in the practice of meditation one encounters tricky knots and convolutions of buried tension that must be worked out and opened; pranayama practice works to develop these advanced relaxation skills while greatly improving body-control and awareness.

In yogic breath retention and deep breathing, the conscious mind exerts a degree of control over the largely unconscious process of respiration; this interaction sheds light on the gap between them, as well as on their essential unity, and is thus a gateway into meditation. Breath retention pulls the mind inward, focusing it onto the still space between the inhalation and the exhalation; this meditative undertow is strengthened by the mind's tendency to mirror the stillness of the breath. The entry point into this kind of meditation is intimate and subjective observation of the internal breathing mechanism, the underlying impulse beneath the inevitable ebb and flow of inhalation and exhalation, which is continually arising from the unconscious and repeatedly translating itself into the physical act of breathing. Thus, ultimately the key element is not *control* of the breath, but rather a deep subjective awareness of its organic process; breath control or breath retention is akin to placing one's hand into a flowing river and feeling the water rush over and through it, thereby experiencing both the river and oneself. In this deep subjective awareness of the breathing process, we find an intimate and concrete connection between consciousness and the physical body. Such introspection is in its essence purely physical; far from looking 'beyond' the body toward some kind of imaginary transcendence, the mind is instead fully present in the moment and completely focused on the physical body and its biological pulsations.

Bhastrika

In contrast to deep breathing and breath retention, bhastrika, or 'breath-of-fire,' is a forceful, rapid breathing technique that actively pumps air in and out of the lungs. While this technique is fairly simple, it is recommended that beginners get some additional instruction if possible; if nothing else, watching a few bhastrika videos will give one a better sense of what it is. Regardless, be careful not to overdo it with this technique; if you start feeling dizzy or lightheaded at any time, you should stop immediately. Breath-of-fire is most often performed from a cross-legged seated position with the spine erect and the hands on the knees, but it can also be used to good effect in combination with virtually any yoga asana and can imbue hatha yoga sessions with an active, stimulating and energetic quality often described as 'heat.' Again, if you have any health conditions or questions about your fitness to practice this technique, please consult a physician before trying it.

Breath-of-fire, or bhastrika, begins with a single deep inhalation, followed by a full exhalation, emptying the lungs. At this point, the abdomen and diaphragm are released and relaxed, which automatically pulls a measure of air back into the lungs as they open, creating a kind of quick, passive, partial inhalation. Note that this is not an active inhalation, but rather a shallow, passive counter-flow of air back into the lungs, as the squeezed-in tension of the exhalation is relaxed. Next, the abdomen is quickly squeezed inward again, in a forceful and audible exhalation. That, in essence, is the entire technique, which

is generally repeated as a freeform sequence of shallow passive inhalations followed immediately by sharp and audible exhalations. The pace of this can vary somewhat, but is generally brisk; a standard interval might be thirty seconds of rapid bhastrika breathing, followed by a minute or so of normal breathing, and then thirty seconds more of bhastrika, followed again by a return to normal breathing.

The key to the breath-of-fire technique is the emphasis on the strong, audible exhalation, powered by the muscular inward squeeze of the abdominal core. The inhalation, by contrast, is passive, silent and shallow; never a sucking of air into the lungs, but merely the passive inverse of the exhalation. Done correctly, breath-of-fire generates a kind of pumping action, as if the lungs were being massaged internally, pushing any stale air from their lower reaches while opening and refreshing them; this can sometimes create a slight tingling sensation of increased oxygenation throughout the body. The rapid squeezing action of the abdominal muscles also makes this a good core exercise, and it is not unusual to experience a bit of soreness in the muscles of the core the next day. Again, in advanced practice bhastrika breathing can be combined with virtually any asana to create an energizing variation in just the same way that this can be done with most of the various deep breathing and breath retention techniques, to good effect.

Understanding the use of breath control is central to the practice of hatha yoga; breath control is one of the best tools in the yoga toolbox for reaching deep into the body, and is an essential element of asana and meditation.

12

LAS VEGAS

We sat facing each other in casual meditation postures, our white cotton feet folded under ourselves on opposing white couches, a metal and glass coffee table extended between us. Beyond the wall of floor-to-ceiling plate glass on my left was the Vegas Strip at night, a pixelated canyon of multicolored lights throbbing and pulsing against the darkness.

'That movie reminded me of Schopenhauer's concept, the Will to Life,' she said.

'Wille zum Leben,' I replied.

'This idea that life is everywhere,' she said. 'That the world is teeming with life, from animals down to the myriad insects and then further down to the vast kingdoms of bacteria and viruses, and that there is somehow something horrible in all this, in this swarming multilayered jungle of life, and in the fact that we are part of it, inescapably joined with it in the most fundamental and most material way.'

'Nietzsche said that Schopenhauer represented a will to nothingness,' I said.

'But they are both really just different sides of the same coin, aren't they' she said. 'Nietzsche, because of his exposure to Darwin, surely understood even better than Schopenhauer that the vitality we notice in snails or worms is essentially the same life force within ourselves, the same life force that our entire civilization has arisen from. Schopenhauer loathed it and pessimistically advocated detachment from what he condescendingly labeled as the 'will to life,' whereas Nietzsche looked ahead to a future higher evolutionary type that would rise up from humanity and transcend it.'

'I'm not sure I see how it's possible for there to be a will to nothingness, though,' I said.

'Well, for one thing, it's certainly not necessary to will nothingness,' she said. 'Nothingness is inescapable; it's found at our very core, in the empty spaces between the structures of our brains, in the gaps between our neurons and the vast spaces between our atoms, and in the gulf of blankness between our subjective perceptions and the reality of the objective world.'

'Then again,' I said, 'if all of space and time is occupied by strings or particles or some kind of energy field, where can nothingness even exist? And for that matter, maybe it doesn't even make sense linguistically to ask if nothingness exists.'

'But we, as conscious subjects, do understand nothingness,' she continued. 'Because we are self-aware, we can conceptualize this idea of nothingness. We exist now, in space and time; at some point in the future, we will no longer exist. The prospect of not existing for a future infinity of time seems like nothingness to us, at least relative to our subjective awareness; the end of consciousness will mean its replacement with nonexistence. If an object external to ourselves ceases to exist, we can see that the rest of existence carries on; but the idea of ceasing to exist as a conscious subject is anticipated as a type of nothingness, because once the subjective basis of our awareness is gone, all of existence as it exists within our perceptions will also be gone. This ultimately infinite and absolute loss of our own selves is perhaps the truest conception of nothingness there is in a universe where nothingness has yet to be found, even in the emptiest voids of outer space.'

'But in a way, we all live on as part of the human species,' I said. 'We are humans more than we are individuals; in a way we're all just tiny pieces of a much larger organism called humanity, petals on a vast flower.'

'Maybe,' she said. 'But from the perspective of subjective consciousness you are entirely separate from the larger organism of humanity. Objectively, yes, you could be viewed as just a part of a vast collective organism, a petal on a flower; but subjectively it is perhaps your misfortune to be awake and fully conscious of your situation, trapped between the impossible prospect of personal destruction, and the inexorable reality of nonexistence.'

'I'm glad that I'm conscious. I enjoy being conscious,' I answered.

'Of course,' she said. 'And, paradoxically, in meditation the idea of nothingness can bring me deep pleasure as well. While meditating I sometimes experience an awareness that I am standing at the brink of an infinity of nothingness, extending far beyond even the deepest depths of my Unconscious; I find this awareness profoundly blissful and deeply soothing somehow. And yet this meditative bliss is experienced only through my body, my own physical life force; nothingness calms and aligns the different levels of my being, allowing me to consciously let go of everything and to relax completely; for me this is always intensely pleasurable.'

13

KUNDALINI & THE CHAKRAS

Kundalini is perhaps the most esoteric and arcane concept in all of yoga. Despite having made its way into certain corners of popular English vernacular, the phrase 'Kundalini yoga' still points toward a subject that is rarely if ever explained in clear and specific terms even by the most experienced of yoga practitioners. Moreover, while artwork and designs based on the symbols of the seven chakras have become a common part of yoga's image in the public mind, frequently showing up on magazine covers and T-shirts and the like, these symbols are actually far more meaningful and complex than most people ever dream. The symbols of the seven chakras are part of an ancient yoga psychology, centered on the idea of individual evolution, which, properly deciphered, contains a litany of insights into the practical experience and progression of yoga meditation. To be clear, we are discussing Kundalini and the chakras here in a strictly symbolic sense; interpreted literally, these concepts are deeply infused with a particularly overbearing brand of mystical thinking, which might be described as a kind of ancient 'science' of mystical anatomy, a peculiar fusion of metaphysics and physiology. At bottom, this kind of mysticism makes no distinction between the domain of the physical world and a kind of transcendent spirituality, and although it is often described as being a form of nondualism, it should properly be understood to be the precise opposite of materialistic nondualism or monism. Traditionally, Kundalini and the chakras are described as physical structures within the human body, but also as 'subtle' or transcendent points of contact that intersect with a spiritual plane or dimension outside of material existence. This peculiar idea, that discrete physical structures within the body called 'chakras' somehow form the nexus points between the physical world and a mystical transcendent realm of supreme consciousness, often presented as something matter-of-fact and unremarkable, a kind of spiritualist trope if you will, is upon closer examination something quite astonishing and outlandish.

Considered carefully, the idea that a series of structures in the body, each a few centimeters wide, whether conceptualized as consisting of nerves or as a kind of subtle 'energy overlay' mapped onto the physical body—or both—could encircle vast terrains of 'cosmic' or divine consciousness within them and could simultaneously be the linchpins that hold the unenlightened soul captive within the 'delusion' of material existence, is anything but matter-of-fact, and resides upon a deep reservoir of mystical supposition. That the purification of these chakras, again somehow existing simultaneously within the body and within a 'soul' or 'subtle body,' could lead to 'liberation,' in the form of an ecstatic and transcendent union between the material and the immaterial aspects of the Supreme Being inside the crown of the head, ultimately mixes up the conceptions of the physical and the metaphysical completely, in a way that is not easy to untangle. While from the perspective of materialism and atheism it might seem easier to simply dispense with these concepts entirely, as being nothing more than part of a beautiful and complex ancient system of mythology, the fact is that Kundalini and the chakras are in fact worth a much closer examination, as some of the root concepts underlying the entire structure of yoga are contained within their symbology.

Materialism centers on the idea that the physical world is real, and that consciousness is rooted in the physical body; since we know that human life was not 'created' and has in fact evolved over hundreds of millions of years, there is no logical reason to believe that such a thing as a 'subtle body' or soul exists, since such a conception stems from the idea that the world is created by a higher power, as a kind of karmic proving ground for playing out the physical embodiment of otherwise undifferentiated and purely immaterial spirit or consciousness. The idea that a 'subtle body' (or soul, or mind, or Ego) could survive death in order to migrate through the realm of the immaterial to reincarnate into a succession of new physical bodies is equally improbable, since all life-forms on Earth are known to be biological and evolved in nature; since we make the assumption that all forms of creationism are false and that life in all of its forms has evolved over eons of time based on the principle of natural selection, the doctrine of reincarnation or 'transmigration' is a logical impossibility, since it presupposes the existence of an elaborately complex design and extension of the natural world. This in turn renders the idea of attaining spiritual 'liberation' from the trap of carnal existence a moot point, as everyone will in the end be 'liberated' from consciousness and material existence in the same inexorable way, by death. Thus, in attempting to make sense of Kundalini and the chakras we must start from the premise that the human body, as the product of an unimaginably long and utterly undetermined process of evolution, cannot possess anything like the underlying divine structure or design that would be necessary for something like the chakras to exist, and must proceed under the assumption that they do not exist in any objective sense of the word. Therefore, the tantric maps and mystical blueprints of the human body that envision it as interlaced with a metaphysical overlay of complex subtle energy channels and chakras, like a kind of mystical miniature-golf course of the soul that every seeker must traverse by penetrating and purifying each luminous spinning cup along its path to liberation, cannot possibly be scientifically accurate or true. It can be decisively demonstrated through anatomical science that the chakras, as conceptualized in tantric literature, do not exist as physical structures within the body; the fact that their traditional anatomical placement may approximate the location of various vital nerve plexuses or ganglia does not alter this fact at all, because the tantric concept of a chakra is vastly different from the idea of a cluster of nerves or blood vessels. From the standpoint of materialism, therefore, the unavoidable fact is that Kundalini and the chakras are in their essence purely symbolic components of tantric mythology, which represent various aspects and characteristics of the human psyche.

From here, Kundalini and the chakras can only be interpreted in purely symbolic or metaphorical terms, as a kind of anatomical mythology that correlates the functionality and structure of the body with the depths of the unconscious mind and attempts to describe its perilous struggle toward consciousness; this tantric description of individual consciousness and evolution is deeply linked to the arts of yoga and meditation. The tantric map of Kundalini and the chakras holds within itself a unique and symmetrical system of symbology, vastly prehistoric in its origins and densely laden with profound psychological meaning. Happily, the detachment and clarity of atheism allows us to freely appreciate the full flower of shaktic Tantra without becoming 'stuck' or otherwise credulously entangled in any of the trappings of faith or spiritualism.

The symbolism of Kundalini reveals within itself a remarkably sophisticated view of human nature, which contains many valuable clues for practitioners of yoga and meditation. The idea of a latent or 'sleeping' energy within the human body or mind that, once 'awakened,' proceeds upward through the spine and begins to pierce the seven chakras, each representing a progressively more advanced and sophisticated level of consciousness, is a powerful symbol of individual mental development. This vision of individual human consciousness as something striving to evolve and pull itself out of the mud in order to claw its way toward self-awareness and maturity, even while resisted and beset at every turn by its own reflexive and unconscious instincts of aggression and fear, resonates with meaning on many levels. Such a view is, in a sense, the polar opposite of the Abrahamic conception of Man as a two-dimensional and serf-like being, somehow created whole and perfect 'in God's image' and yet still abjectly unfortunate and brutal—and presumably incapable of further evolution. This Judeo-Christian conception of Man as a thoroughly extroverted creature, completely defined by the superficial characteristics of race, sex and tribe and suited only for the supine and absolute worship of a divine king, stands in stark contrast to the idea of progressive inner evolution put forth by Tantra.

Kundalini and the chakras have been described in various works of tantric literature, including the Sat-Cakra-Nirupana and the Padaka-Pancaka, which were famously translated into English in the early 1900s by Sir Arthur Avalon and published in his book The Serpent Power. Many of the esoteric concepts in these works are thought to have their origins in the ancient goddess cults of South India and most likely predate the Rig Veda by many thousands of years. Avalon's translations and analysis have become a kind of touchstone for modern students of Tantra, and have helped many westerners to better understand the underlying concepts and philosophies of Kundalini yoga as it is encountered in various modern ashrams and schools. These concepts, however, are easy to misinterpret at face value, and have frequently been partially assimilated into various half-baked popular notions of the 'subtle energy body' or the supposed oneness of 'spiritual' or 'transcendent' energy with various parts of human physical anatomy. Such connections have wound their way into the modern English vernacular through, for example, various clichés about the energy of the heart chakra, or of 'seeing' through the Third Eye, and so forth. The psychologist Carl Jung warned that these tantric concepts and symbols have a peculiar 'clinging' or infectious quality about them, which for some reason makes them particularly attractive to the unconscious mind. Jung was concerned that these concepts could be, as he put it, especially 'dangerous' for westerners, who might lack the cultural background to properly contextualize them, and he cautioned that they are often readily accepted and internalized but are at the same time difficult to truly get one's mind around or to unlearn, having a tendency to adhere tenaciously to one's concept of self or unconscious body-image. In a series of lectures given in the 1930s, Jung said that the chakras are, correctly understood, a symbolic representation of the human psyche and a map of its potential development, the larger part of which is always, like an iceberg, submerged below the surface of consciousness. In Jung's explanation, Kundalini symbolizes the unconscious mind, as it begins to 'wake up' to itself through the process of deep reflection and introspection, and gradually begins to push its way out of its embryonic shell of robotic instinct and move toward self-awareness.

Each of the various chakras is associated with a specific area of the body and signifies a particular level of mental and emotional development. This in a sense invites us to view the entire human body as symbolic, with the lower abdomen symbolizing the basic instinctual drives related to procreation and defecation, the central abdomen and belly symbolizing the potentially fierce emotional instincts of survival, nourishment and social conformity and the higher latitudes of the chest, throat and head symbolizing progressively higher and more abstract levels of consciousness and mental development. The symbolism of each chakra is thus integrally related to the physical and psychological significance of its bodily location—the genital region, for example, or the throat—and is in a sense a condensation or crystallized reflection of the unconscious mind's innate understanding of the body. Each chakra contains interwoven layers of symbolic meaning, hinting at the key for 'rising' to the next body region or level and its correspondingly higher level of mental development; 'rising' in this sense symbolizes an increase in self-awareness and a more complete integration of the unconscious mind and the physical body with the conscious Ego, allowing for greater inner freedom to act creatively and to respond to stimuli in conscious and intelligent ways, rather than reflexively, robotically or mechanically.

In its traditional tantric conception, Kundalini is described as a small but immensely powerful reservoir of subtle energy that lies dormant in the human body, coiled like a serpent at the base of the spine. According to tradition, this latent energy, upon being awakened either through intense yogic exercise or by the affectionate gaze of a Kundalini master, begins to stir and to subsequently proceed upward through the spine, gradually purifying and piercing the sequence of seven chakras along the way. As Kundalini works its way upward, it in a sense pulls an individual's subjective consciousness into and eventually through each chakra, awakening and purifying it of 'samskaras,' the otherwise indelible traces of past 'karmas' or actions, and transmuting the chakra from an obstacle into a source of spiritual strength, thereby allowing the aspirant to rise higher toward 'enlightenment.' A yogi is thus thought to 'rise' to successively higher levels of personal spiritual development, a process that eventually culminates in a kind of mystical union between the 'masculine' element of cosmic consciousness and the 'feminine' element of universal being and manifestation, inside the final chakra, Sahasrara, at the top of the skull. The culmination of this mystical union essentially undoes the individual, resulting in the state of liberation or nirvana—a permanent and supremely blissful transcendence of earthly existence. This is again the traditional tantric conception of Kundalini, as described in the Sat-Cakra-Nirupana and various other tantric sutras.

In Jung's view, Kundalini symbolizes the unconscious mind. The latent power of the unconscious is characterized as a serpent-like human power that sleeps, dormant and unknown, at the very root of an individual's physical and mental self at the base of the spine. Kundalini's 'awakening' and its subsequent ascent symbolize the gradual and deep stirrings of self-awareness within the individual, fueled by the deep introspection and inner silence of meditation, which gradually decipher and unlock the unconscious or robotic mechanisms of the personality and the Ego, thereby releasing a flood of surplus mental energy and unleashing the mind from its preprogrammed patterns of conformity and reaction.

Muladhara

The first chakra described in the Sat-Cakra-Nirupana is the Muladhara chakra, also known as the root chakra; it is traditionally located near the base of the spine, at roughly the same latitude as the anus. Muladhara is traditionally associated with the earth element and symbolizes a state of mental development where introspection and cognitive self-awareness are completely lacking, where one is in a sense unaware of consciousness and of the existence of the mind, seeing only outward and thinking only in terms of externalities. At this level of development an individual cannot see beyond the surface appearance of things and is trapped in a world of solid objects, with no way to penetrate deeper into the shiny puzzle of existence. In the practice of meditation, this is the level of the beginner, who tries to meditate by repeatedly sitting in silence with his or her eyes closed trying to find the door 'into' meditation while remaining cognitively external to the entire process, dryly wondering whether meditation has occurred and whether meditation is in fact even something real.

Oddly, many of the most sincerely religious individuals seem stuck at precisely this psychological level, which we might characterize as a state of being 'locked out' of reflective self-awareness, a place where even prayer becomes primarily an externalized activity, often nothing more than an outward gesture performed largely for the sake of conformity. This stage of mental development is also often characterized by a keen awareness of racial, sexual and cultural differences, and an exaggerated adherence to ritual and propriety, along with a strong tendency toward unquestioning, blind obedience. The tendency to discriminate against people based solely on race or sex, in particular, evinces an inability to see anything in people beyond their outward physical characteristics; this obviously unconscious tribal tendency to unavoidably and relentlessly 'judge books by their cover,' so to speak, demonstrates not just a lack of empathy for other human beings, but also hints at a profound lack of self-awareness. The individual who can only see outward necessarily perceives the world as completely solid and opaque and inevitably fails to see consciousness in others, thereby also conceiving of 'God' in precisely the same way, as a solid and material 'king in the sky,' for example, who rules through raw material power and vengeance and whose prophecy will be 'realized' when he physically returns to Earth. Lacking self-consciousness, individuals at this level can sometimes be manipulated into acting like little more than mechanical objects, unable to think for themselves and constantly requiring clear-cut boundaries and guidelines for their behavior.

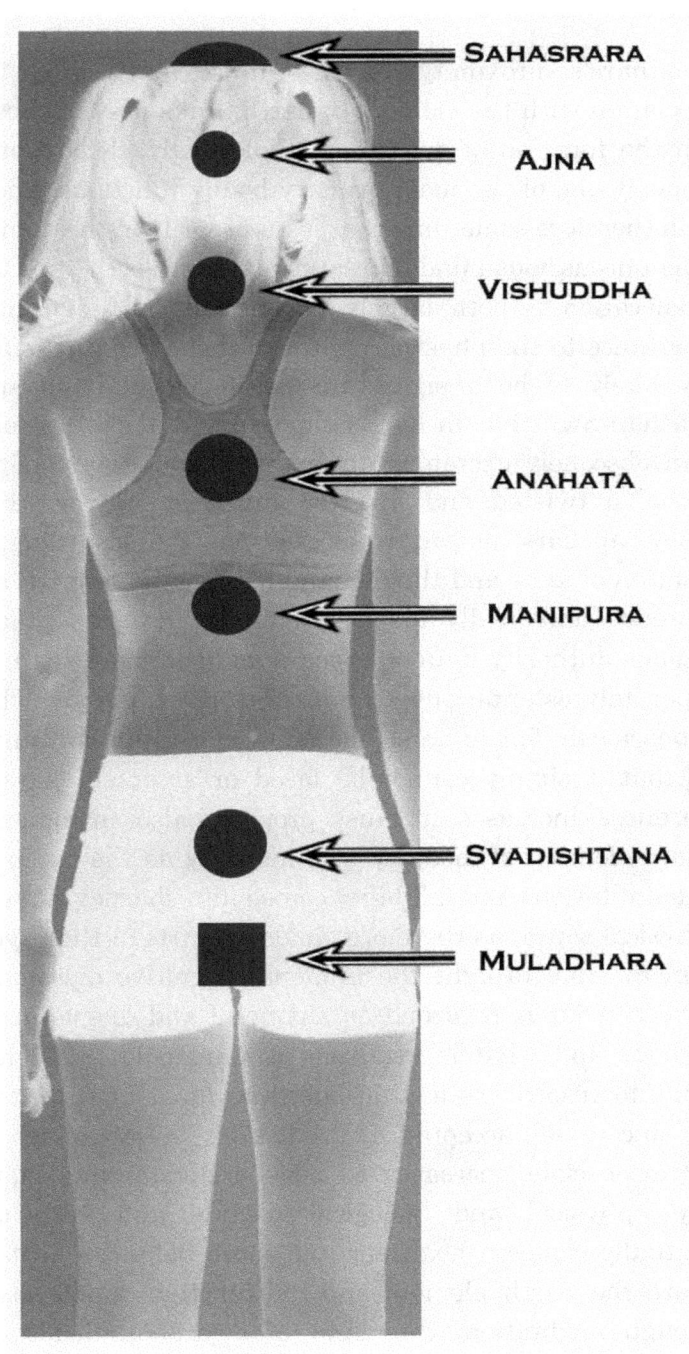

Muladhara's proximity to the anus, as well as its association with the element of earth, links it symbolically with the function of defecation. Biologically, defecation is obviously one of the most primary bodily functions, and is again therefore something that is necessarily in the domain of the unconscious mind to a large extent; that the function of defecation is both largely unconscious and of central importance to the physical organism means that it is also very likely to be a significant psychological blind spot. Jonathan Swift has in his writings hinted at the presence of an obscenely excretory unconscious underworld of the psyche, a twisted and inverted funhouse mirror where money appears as an analogue for the hoarding or retention of feces and the demand for gravity, respect, and reverence universally insisted upon by government and religious authority figures appears as little more than the desperately ostentatious attempt to conceal that which is unconsciously felt to be so shameful and filthy within the self that it simply cannot be faced or accepted. As self-awareness increases it must properly also introduce a certain element of modesty and humility as the extent of one's limitations and fallibility comes into sharper focus; in a physical sense, as the more shadowy parts of the psyche begin to come to light the immense cognitive dissonance between what is regarded as shameful and disgusting in the body and what is idealized as immaculate and holy begins to resolve itself, thus allowing for a more relaxed and sincere self-acceptance. Predictably, as awareness of the unconscious increases so does understanding of the body's physical and biological nature, and with this eventually comes a healthier and more balanced attitude toward the 'earth' element and the function of defecation. Through meditation, this kind of awareness leads one toward a kinder and more sincere affection for the body, which does not require any awkward lurching between the polarities of grotesquely ashamed self-loathing and righteously hysterical self-glorification.

At the level of Muladhara, consciousness is, metaphorically speaking, in a sleeping or dormant state; awareness is focused outward and an individual is often completely self-identified with whatever society or group it has been born into, and sees no reason to penetrate more deeply into the riddle of its own existence. We could thus say that Muladhara symbolizes the most primitive level of the human psyche, where the seed of consciousness lies buried beneath feet of solid concrete, unaware of its own nature and potential; through the process of introspective meditation, however, various earthquakes and disruptions may begin to occur, upsetting the applecart of mundane superficiality and offering various hints and clues that something else is lurking below.

Svadishtana

The next chakra in the tantric pantheon is called Svadhishtana, which is located along the spine at the approximate latitude of the genital region and is associated with the element of water. Svadhishtana symbolizes a level of mental development where the individual has started to become more conscious of the existence of the psyche and has begun to awaken to its depth, beginning at times to gaze into down it as it looks back recursively into itself.

The level symbolized by Svadishtana could be described as a kind of adolescence of the psyche where the mind of the meditator becomes increasingly transparent to itself, but at the same time suffers from certain growing pains and instabilities, as the firm emotional ground of its solid base at times seems to dissolve into nothingness. As this new awareness unfolds, an individual may feel troubled by the power of the imagination and somewhat lost at sea, afraid of losing control of the mind or of losing the self altogether. This is a vulnerable stage of development, where the individual can feel overly sensitive and prone to anxiety or compulsiveness and can suffer from a general lack of identity and self-trust. The meditator, in other words, having finally stumbled onto the existence of the mind now senses its unknown depths and the dark, deep-sea jungles extending far below the thin ice of normal consciousness. From this seemingly unstable and untenable position, the task of trusting in one's inner equilibrium enough to truly relax and submerge into tranquil meditation may appear terrible and gargantuan.

Svadhishtana chakra is symbolically correlated with the genital region and the sexual instincts; as the mind begins to discover itself in this turbulent adolescent stage of meditation it must inevitably confront the high-voltage inner tensions of its own sexual desire, insecurity and shame, eventually finding a way to surrender the firewall of repression and come to a point of conscious balance and self-acceptance, integrating sexuality with the conscious psyche in an open and healthy way. Conversely, when sexual feelings are blocked and repressed and their powerful biological and emotional energy is shunted sideways, the personality can become twisted, whole areas of the mind and the body walled off from consciousness by painful feelings of guilt and soul-numbing shockwaves of anxiety and insecurity. Such brutalizing internal balkanization and conflict, where many of the mind's most delicate flowers must necessarily be smashed down and paved over, can lead to a plethora of compulsions, complexes and obsessions, which frantically seek out patterns, words and rituals with which to mask the stark unpleasantness of their underlying tension and cognitive dissonance. When such compulsive tendencies are combined with superstition and magical thinking—the belief that one's own thoughts and wishes have the power to directly cause outcomes and events in the real world—the result can be powerful forms of anxious obsession and compulsion, fueled by paroxysms of solipsistic mental self-preoccupation and desperate self-loathing, where the mind becomes trapped into repetitively fighting with itself.

At the Swadishtana level of meditation, the rejection of superstition and magical thinking is absolutely vital for the mind, and is a necessary condition for unconditional trust and faith in oneself. In meditation the mind must be allowed to roam freely and one must be able to look inward fearlessly and with an attitude of equanimity. In all of this, the relaxed and unconditional acceptance of one's own sexuality is crucial; the shameful and compulsive repression of instinctive sexual urges and emotions serves no purpose in yoga or meditation, and is in fact a significant obstacle to inner transparency. The powerful forces of sexuality are a central and undeniable aspect of the psyche's natural landscape and a meditator must be able to face them squarely and make inner peace; the nature of the individual self must be understood and accepted in all of its vicissitudes in order to progress toward inner equanimity and balance. In meditation, unseen icebergs of inner psychological conflict have a way of rising up as formidable foes against focus and concentration, coagulating into sticky and unavoidable obsessions that demand resolution, like trolls asking for answers to riddles at bridge crossings. The honest student of meditation has no choice but to patiently untangle and interpret these scary and urgent psychic puzzles, which are so often intimately intertwined with the deepest fabric of the Ego and can seem to threaten its self-image and self-esteem. For the sake of maintaining internal clarity and integrity without generalized sexual repression or a lazy reliance on the robotic and unconscious rules of morality, which condemn even as they forbid, it is necessary to carefully work through all of one's 'issues' during meditation. An ability to find the subtle keys of self-understanding within oneself during meditation, or to pick the intricate locks of painful and difficult emotions, can unlock deep streams of creative mental bandwidth and energy.

As illustrated in the Sat-Cakra-Nirupana, the traditional image of Svadhishtana contains a sea monster or leviathan within it. Jung says that this is highly significant symbolically, the leviathan representing an ominous danger to the emerging self, deep within the unconscious mind. This imagery is also suggestive of the brain's reptilian complex, the most primitive part of the Triune Brain model, the primitive and largely instinctual core segment of the human nervous system that consists of the spinal cord and the basal ganglia. According to the Triune Brain hypothesis, the reptilian complex is devoid of emotion and empathy, and concerns itself solely with eating, fighting, survival, dominance, aggression, ritual display, territoriality and reproduction. In a sense, the image of the leviathan within Svadhishtana represents precisely this primal and potentially dangerous aspect of the unconscious mind, the invisible source of the conscious Ego's unarticulated fears of losing itself to the dark mirror it sees at its own core. Although it would be nice to say here that meditation is always easy and that there are never any unpleasant shadows within the mind, the fact is that human nature is extremely complex and multifaceted, interwoven with layers of our animal legacy at every level; it is also fair to say that these more biologically primitive aspects of the self are in every sense completely integral to the 'higher' parts of human nature as well, and cannot be simply repressed or discarded. Eventually an advanced meditator has no choice but to navigate the difficult waters that lie between the rational and the irrational parts of the mind, at times encountering the least evolved aspects of human nature but with an understanding that what can be brought into the light of consciousness might also be also transmuted through reason and self-love into something valuable and energetic, which can be safely integrated with the personality. The healthy expansion of conscious self-awareness into the more unconscious regions of the mind can thus attenuate one's worst emotional tendencies and reactions and can serve as an inoculation against the reflexive and reactive mind viruses that so easily infect large population groups in the forms of fascism, group psychosis, fear, irrationality, racial prejudice, tribalism, extreme nationalism, and the uncontrolled savagery and slaughter of war. As a yogi begins to attain composure and balance in meditation at the level symbolized by Svadishtana, the initial stormy difficulties begin to clarify and subside, and meditation is increasingly experienced as a cooling, calming, healing and even blissful practice.

Manipura chakra

The next chakra is called Manipura and is generally located along the inner spine in the area of the solar plexus. Manipura is symbolically correlated with the element of fire, and is often regarded as a difficult and perilous location on the journey of meditation, where the emotions of fear and anger must be confronted and resolved. Jung describes an interesting metaphorical connection between the element of fire and the power of digestion, and points out that as traditionally drawn in ancient tantric art Manipura contains a symbol within it that resembles a cooking pot or crucible of some kind; based on the fact that humans have uniquely evolved the practice of cooking their food before eating it, Jung draws a symbolic thread between the element of fire and the process of digestion, likening the cooking of food to a kind of external process of pre-digestion. As eating and the conversion of food into energy is a fundamental biological process at the core of all animal life, the distinctly human externalization of this process into the culinary arts is significant; the symbolism of Manipura, with a crucible of fire, heat, and physical transformation at its center, is evocative of the deep unconscious linkage between the raw biological instincts and the practical intellect, which long ago learned to survive by changing the world around it. It should not, of course, surprise us that there is always an underlying unconscious constellation of purely biological behaviors and attitudes clustered around food and the acts of cooking and eating, because at bottom these things form such a central nexus between our human and our animal natures. The difficulty that many people have in controlling their hunger or weight, for example, is just one example of the obvious fact that regulating the body's instinct to eat is something that is frequently beyond direct conscious control.

If you have ever seen a group of cats or dogs at feeding time, you might have observed that they tend to get a bit more serious or aggressive when the food comes out. This is natural and completely forgivable in pets, and can even be a source of charm and amusement; the same behavior in people, however, is universally regarded as rude and offensive. While waiting in line at a food court, supermarket or buffet, it is possible to notice that the presence or scarcity of food can sometimes cause people to become a bit more tense, pushy and aggressive than they might otherwise be. When hungry people are pressed into tight proximity with each other, especially in 'first come, first served' scenarios where there is an element of uncertainty involved, the instinctual impulses rooted in the belly can become more urgent; the occasional brief and relatively moderate eruptions of rudeness or over-assertiveness that can result, and the stiff static of emotional tension that often permeates such situations, is in a sense a vestigial remnant of an evolutionary legacy left over from the endless struggle for food that our countless ancestors have survived. The tendency toward aggression and territoriality when food and hunger are involved is one reason good table manners are so highly valued everywhere, and are considered essential in sophisticated company; it is also why teaching children to be polite, and to share and be courteous during meals, is a fundamental step in childrearing and primary education.

At the level of what Jung refers to in his lectures as 'Manipura consciousness,' the meditator starts to become more self-conscious and aware of the bodily instincts constellated around feeding, self-preservation and territoriality; in the light of this increasing sensitivity, the adrenal emotions of fear and anger come into sharper focus and appear somewhat differently than they did before. On bad days they may seem to loom menacingly over the subjective mental vista, making life appear more adversarial, difficult, stressful and chaotic than it actually is. Once the process of meditation has begun, however, the only way out is through; instinctive impulses that in less reflective persons have already been trained or balanced into a 'normal' personality must be consciously faced and manually reintegrated into a broader understanding of the self. In the long run this is a highly worthwhile endeavor, as the same emotional energies that fuel determination, industriousness, bravery, loyalty, ambition and motivation are also capable of manifesting in their more negative forms as rage, resentment, hatred and fear, which can eventually seep into the body's emotional water supply in the form of chronic stress, depression and unhappiness. Coming to terms with the nature and mechanisms of this visceral spectrum of emotion is a crucial part of progressing in meditation at this stage of the process.

Symbolically, Manipura's placement at the center of the body in the solar plexus region is very significant. The connection between breathing and emotion is well known: anger, fear and sadness tend to cause tight, shallow and constricted breathing, whereas happiness, kindness, empathy and relaxation tend to lead toward deeper, more expansive breathing. In some sense, these emotions are almost identical with their associated breathing patterns; many yoga instructors understand this from experience, and know that stress and emotional turmoil cannot coexist with deep relaxed breathing and that these emotions begin to dissolve the instant one starts slowing down and deepening the breath. There is also a strong physiological connection between the stomach and the emotions of stress: excess adrenaline, fear, anger, worry, shame and resentment, in sufficient doses and concentrations, can be a more or less direct cause of indigestion, acid reflux, compulsive overeating and even ulcers. In fact, stress, fear and anger are often so powerfully felt in the stomach and abdomen that many people implicitly seem to feel that these emotions actually originate there; conversely, the happy and relaxed emotions such as love, friendship, fearlessness and confidence tend to soothe the abdomen and make it feel warm and comforted; such good experiences are often expressed with phrases such as 'what a wonderful dinner party,' or 'that was the most enjoyable meal I have ever had in my life,' and so forth.

Many common euphemisms hint at the central symbolic importance of the abdomen: a brave man 'has guts,' or 'has the stomach' for a difficult or unpleasant task, while a coward may be said to be 'gutless' or yellow-bellied, an unconscious reference to the excessive bile of jaundice. Shame, embarrassment, jealousy and violent rage are often experienced directly in the belly, and ancient Japanese samurai who had suffered disgrace or dishonor were known to kill themselves by ripping open their own abdomens with a short sword in the practice of seppuku, which sought to avoid disgrace and to honor the subjective relationships of rank, fidelity and loyalty above personal physical existence. Many Asian martial arts revolve around cultivating and strengthening the power of the abdomen through various breathing and centering techniques, and a master of Karate or Judo is awarded the 'black belt,' a symbol of courage, expertise and strong character. A top prizefighter wears a championship belt around his waist, signifying strength, skill and winning mettle, and the warrior who has been mortally stabbed on the battlefield, his abdomen pierced by an enemy sword, is finished in the most unequivocal and primal manner, the Gordian knot of his physical power and existence irrevocably cut. Meanwhile, in the safety of their warm beds, the innocent sleeping bellies of happy babies can be observed to rise and fall with their breathing in the most sublimely relaxed and supple way.

Manipura symbolizes, and the abdomen embodies, profoundly material and biological instincts that play a constant role in human psychology. We find these instincts at play everywhere, sublimated and woven into the tapestry of everyday life, and yet at the same time we do well to remember that in their raw and unadulterated primal manifestations they can be extremely dangerous. In his lectures on Kundalini, Jung discussed his experiences with native tribes while traveling in Kenya, and talks at length about the absolute adherence and strict attention to symbolic social rituals that was required within their social circles. Jung describes these rigid social customs and manners as a type of safeguard or protection against the unconscious instinctual drives of anger and aggression, which can run amok when traditional standards of societal order, custom and politeness break down, resulting in violence or, on a larger scale, even war; we see shades of such foresighted social prophylaxes in the Western custom of shaking hands, for example, and in the rigid hierarchies of military rank and salutation that form such a major part of aristocratic republican etiquette; it is also clearly on view in Asian countries, in such traditional courtesies as the bowing of the head during greetings and so forth.

Jung's point seems to be that the tribesmen instinctively understand there is something delicate and very dangerous in their social relationships and interactions with other men; their awareness of this potential for danger may not be articulated or consciously understood, perhaps not having manifested or been seen in its worst forms for generations, but it has nonetheless made its way into their tribal wisdom and customs across the distance of time in the form of social rules and customs that are observed with the utmost seriousness. For those sitting within the social circle of such a tribe, adherence to these rules and rituals is of the highest significance, their familiar structures and courtesies a kind of talisman to ward off what Jung describes as the dangerous 'explosions' of emotion and human violence that are possible when misunderstanding, jealousy, fear, disrespect and anger unexpectedly rear their ugly heads. In such circumstances it can be considered a grave breach of manners to break the rules of tradition and ritual; failing to accept a ceremonial gift or offering of food, for instance, can arouse dangerous suspicion and animus, when simply accepting it would have opened the door to an outpouring of friendliness and hospitality. Such a ritualistic offering openly invites one into the group's inner circle of friendliness; by graciously accepting such a customary offering one also accepts and acknowledges one's place as a guest within the tribal circle, and thus assures everyone involved that the danger of violence and treachery is not present. To reject or insult the ritual or customs of the group can rapidly change warm and welcoming friendliness into an inexorable group immune response of fear, dislike, alarm, and outrage. In Jung's description of the Kenyan tribes there are various clues as to why religious societies and groups so often value conformity, obedience and ritual; even if, in practice, such conformity and adherence to ritual seems like little more than mimicry or obligatory repetition devoid of any actual feeling or meaning it may still be regarded within the unconscious logic of a group as something of the utmost significance, since any group must necessarily define itself in terms of insiders and outsiders, members and nonmembers, 'us' and 'them.'

In meditation, the level of Manipura symbolizes the struggle of consciousness to come to terms with the body's potential for energy, action and emotion in the midst of the highly charged complexities and stark dangers of the material world. Through the process of meditation and progressive relaxation one develops a measure of conscious understanding and control over many emotional impulses and reactions that might otherwise occur altogether reflexively and unconsciously; the experience of meditation gives one an extra level of self-monitoring and self-perception, which can at times serve as a firewall against rash impulsivity. Breathing techniques in particular are extremely important at this stage, as learning to control one's breathing, even in the most difficult or strenuous situations, increases mastery of the physical body and the ability to consciously manage the physiological 'fight-or-flight' response. Accomplished yoga practitioners are able to 'rise above' emotional stress by recognizing that physiological feelings and responses are not the same thing as thoughts, feelings and mental states; they are thus better able to defuse stress or negative emotion on a purely physical level, without necessarily feeling compelled to untangle it mentally, or to replay a stressful stimulus repeatedly within the mind, vainly searching for a better or more satisfying outcome.

Yoga has a well-deserved reputation for being a powerful and deeply relaxing method of relieving stress, however mere physical relaxation can only take you so far; in seeking to remain relaxed and stress-free in what often seems to be an inherently stressful and even hostile and dangerous world, one's own impulses toward selfishness, aggression, hostility, insecurity and fear must also be confronted, and one must gain a greater freedom from the reflexive inner mechanisms of emotional cause and effect. Acquiring the inner detachment, perspective and control to truly let go of anger and fear can allow one to bypass the damaging physical and emotional tension caused by chronic stress; as the mind becomes less burdened and afflicted with excess quantities of adrenaline, cortisol and other stress hormones, higher and more delicate levels of mental functioning are more easily maintained. The challenge for the meditator is to not suppress or water-down emotions like anger or fear, but rather to directly experience and examine them as they occur, using meditative discrimination to trace their origins and 'rise above' them mentally while at the same time working to defuse and attenuate them with the physical techniques of yogic breath control and relaxation.

Anahata chakra
Proceeding upward, the next chakra in the sequence is called Anahata, also known as the heart chakra, which is symbolically linked to the element of air. The heart chakra signifies individual consciousness that has reached a level of mental maturity capable of differentiating itself from its instincts and reflexive emotional reactions and has begun to identify itself with the higher angels of its own more refined and abstract mental faculties. Prior to reaching this level of development an individual is more often than not completely identified mentally with his or her feelings and emotions, as the vivid hues of the emotional spectrum can so easily color the clear water of consciousness. The powerfully reflexive mechanisms of emotion, which extend

all the way down to the foundations of the nervous system, are easily capable of overwhelming consciousness and the higher neocortical components of the brain, resulting in mental identification with feelings and emotions, a sense that the physiological sensations of emotion are emerging from within the Ego and the mind, and are in fact a true expression of the inner mental self. This dynamic is reflected in language also, for instance in the usage of the verb 'to be'—what Korzybski refers to as the 'is of identity,' which is observable in phrases such as 'I am angry' or 'I am afraid,' where linguistically the subject is being completely identified with a feeling or state.

As one begins to see past this reflexive unity of emotion, feeling and identity, it becomes easier to identify with consciousness and abstract intelligence instead; the self begins to reveal itself as something subtler and more mercurial, a quality of reason and consciousness that is naturally detached and superior to the emotions, and is able to view them from an abstract perspective and exert a certain level of control over them. At this stage an individual meditator can more easily observe an emotion such as anger as it is occurring in real-time, experiencing it as a feeling and a set of physiological responses while remaining detached from it; this ability to 'witness' one's own feeling of anger without becoming identified with it can allow one to step outside the state of 'being angry,' so to speak, and thus sidestep the self-perpetuating cycle of becoming progressively angrier at the fact that one 'is angry.' This is a crucial breakthrough, one that implies the existence of an abstract 'I' of reason and self-possession above the level of the emotions; even under the ferocious pressure of strong emotional stimulation, the mind on some level remains capable of detachment, because it has become identified with the higher constellations of abstract reasoning and intelligence.

Jung considered this transition toward self-consciousness and away from identification with the feelings and physical instincts of the body to be highly significant, a crucial step in the evolutionary development of the individual symbolized by the dividing line of the solar plexus, which separates the human torso into two distinct regions, upper and lower. Below the barrier of the solar plexus are found the viscera and the organs of gross digestion, while above it are the heart and the lungs, capable of transmuting the subtle element of oxygen into the energy required for consciousness and life, as well as the head and throat, which encompass the organs of speech and thought. The element of air thus symbolizes the subtle and ethereal nature of the subjective mental realm of thought, perception and imagination; in the metaphorical context of Kundalini yoga, it indicates a progressively more rarefied state of being, the result of moving further into the purely conceptual realm of. the intellect or 'buddhi.' Sigmund Freud once said '*The voice of reason is soft. But it is very persistent.*' Anahata, or the heart, symbolizes in shaktic Tantra the place where that quiet voice of reason begins to be distinctly heard, and where consciousness and self-awareness begin to grow noticeably stronger.

Vishuddha chakra

The next chakra, Vishuddha, is located in the throat region and corresponds to the mythical element of ether. In the ancient symbology of the five elements—earth, water, fire, air and ether—the element of ether represents that which is in a sense more subtle and rarefied than air and is called psyche or spirit, the ineffable mind-stuff of consciousness and subjectivity. Vishuddha symbolizes a level of mental development where concepts, abstractions and imagination begin to weigh more than the 'external' world of matter and objects, and is reached with the budding awareness that all of one's perceptions and internal maps of reality exist nowhere else but within the mind. This is, potentially, the realm of unrestricted imagination and creativity, where the unmoored mind can drag the malleable constructs of the intellect and the imagination into the territories of the uncharted and the undefined. At this level a meditator has become keenly aware of the impenetrable gulf between subjective awareness and objective reality and is thus paradoxically *more* aware than before of the world's essential material reality and substance. Pratyahara, or the withdrawal of the senses in meditation, now comes more easily, as the meditator begins to recognize that the immense flow of mental energy and stimulation pouring in through the senses is ultimately generated by the nervous system itself rather than the outside world, and can therefore be controlled. As it becomes increasingly clear through meditation that sense perception is a purely mental process of abstraction that occurs within the brain, it also becomes apparent that this process is in some sense similar to the way that memories, dreams and imaginings are processed and mediated in the mind; this awareness tends to make one progressively more rigorous and scientific in all of one's endeavors and more keenly aware of the probability of human error or misperception in every situation. This evolution parallels in some sense the mental leap from living only in what is known as the 'naked-eye' universe, to 'seeing' or conceptualizing the universe in terms of the abstract concepts of physical cosmology, chemistry, and quantum physics.

Again, ironically at this stage an advanced meditator is actually more in touch with physical reality and therefore with the body; not only freer in meditation to traverse the mind's internal maps of the body, but also increasingly aware of the realm of pure objective physicality just outside the reach of conscious awareness. As subjective awareness nudges like a blind worm against the physical enclosure of the nervous system inside meditation, it may gradually through force of will dig down closer to the bodily roots of consciousness; this results in a progressive 'downward' linking during meditation into the more primitive reptilian regions of the nervous system, consciousness centering for a time in the billion year old lower reaches of the brain stem and the spinal cord. This ability to switch gears and link conscious awareness downward into raw corporeality allows a meditator to relax more deeply, submerging into trancelike thought-free mental states of animal equipoise that can soothe, recharge, release and rejuvenate the upper levels of the mind like nothing else. A yoga practitioner who works as a software engineer, for example, might be able to write meticulous computer code for twelve solid hours during the day, maintaining a laser-like mental focus the whole time, and yet after work be capable of effortlessly 'switching off' and relaxing, communing deeply with the physical body and transitioning easily into carefree and detached meditation or yogic sleep. With open access to the deep waters of the unconscious and the ability to consciously disengage the mind from thoughts and mental processes, an advanced yoga practitioner develops a nose for finding his or her own inner well of blissful relaxation and mental replenishment, and doesn't need drugs or alcohol to unwind or 'let go.'

Ajna chakra and Sahasrara chakra

The final two chakras are Ajna chakra, located roughly between the eyebrows and often referred to as the 'third eye,' and Sahasrara, located at the top of the head and often referred to as the 'thousand petaled lotus.' The Sat-Cakra-Nirupana describes Kundalini as eventually ascending into the seventh and last chakra, Sahasrara, and thereupon reaching an apex of cosmic bliss and an ecstatic mystical union with the Supreme Being, resulting directly in the 'liberation' and complete enlightenment of the individual yogi or meditator. Traditionally, Kundalini is often represented as a female power or goddess, the dark side of Maya's power of manifestation that upon awakening begins to unravel the illusion of material existence from within the individual mind; upon reaching the pinnacle of Sahasrara and consummating her union with the symbolically male power of pure consciousness, or Shiva, Kundalini merges with it completely, thus undoing entirely the various knots of material existence and bringing about the irreversible liberation of nirvana—the merging and dissolution of the individual stream of personal consciousness into a cosmic ocean of divine super-consciousness. Within the context of this tantric mythology Ajna chakra, or the Third Eye, is a kind of way station at the border between individual Ego-based consciousness below, and Sahasrara's ocean of cosmic light above; thus the path through Ajna chakra is sometimes described as being blocked by fear, or by the instinctive hesitation to relinquish individual existence and rise unsupported up into the immensely vast and high-domed inner ceiling of Sahasrara.

Symbolically these two chakras, the 'head chakras' if you will, might be interpreted as signifying successively higher and more advanced levels of self-awareness and intellect. Jung, for his part, hesitates to describe the symbolism of these two chakras at all, stating instead that they perhaps hint, in an anthropological sense, at a further evolutionary horizon of human development that we cannot at present see or conceptualize. In my experience, many yoga practitioners and meditators get stuck or hung up on the tantric descriptions and mythology of these charkas, and on the stories of dramatic meditation 'experiences' given by those who have supposedly ascended to them, and as a result wind up with the erroneous expectation that 'reaching the head' in meditation is a very rare experience, which would, should it ever happen, be marked by terrifying visions, thunderous sounds, kaleidoscopic showers of mystical light and so forth. In reality, it should be apparent that one's head or brain is always the seat and center of any meditation and thus, conceptually, the rarefied realms of 'Ajna' and 'Sahasrara' are never far-off remote destinations, but are in fact always intimately close and familiar to all of us at all times. The experience of advanced meditation is therefore never the spectacular 'rocket to the Moon' of mystical enlightenment that many yogis imagine or fear, but rather the experience of something very real within the mental world that is available to everyone—something that is already present at every moment and may open itself by subtle degrees as the practice of genuine meditation deepens.

From the perspective of the individual, eventually everything comes to an end, each life and its subjective universe inevitably collapsing down to a single point of nothingness at the moment of death. The classical yoga concept of nirvanic liberation in a sense mirrors this fact, as logically speaking the annihilation of individual consciousness would necessarily result from any absolute merging into some kind of cosmic or divine; while this idea can be viewed from several angles, what is interesting here is that nirvana is some sense then a metaphorical analogue for death, since in both death and nirvana the surrender and loss of individuality is absolute and unconditional. Thus, in considering the symbolic significance of Sahasrara within the system of Kundalini yoga, as being the seventh and final chakra in the progression and physically representative of 'liberation' both in and from the body, we see that it is necessarily linked to the idea of death. This is a very meaningful piece of Tantra's psychological roadmap for meditation; an acute awareness of one's personal mortality, and even a certain preoccupation with death, is an inevitable stage in the meditative process. A yoga practitioner, even one who may have actually begun the practice of yoga solely for the pursuit of increased health, youth and physical longevity, eventually begins to realize that there is nothing solid or secure inside of space and time, and that death is an inexorable and inescapable reality. What was once imagined in the third-person as an impossible and grotesque fantasy now begins to take shape in the mind not as the mere destruction of the body, but as the absolute loss of one's unique individual conscious self into an infinite ocean of time. This acute awareness of one's inevitable end, along with the contemplation of an infinity of nonexistence, can itself become an obstacle to further progress in yoga; the challenge for the yogi at this stage of development is to continue in the practice of meditation, balancing detachment with a sincere quality of fascination and self-love and pushing onward in the shadow of oblivion, like a lone climber ascending a frozen mountain on Mars, lost among the vast reaches of geologic time with no hope of ever returning home.

If one practices yoga and meditation long enough, eventually one encounters the necessity of having to let go of oneself completely. This is, ultimately, perhaps what is symbolized by Sahasrara: the undefined object of meditation that is completely beyond the brain's galaxy of neural connections—sheer nothingness. Within the unconscious mind there lies concealed a surprising capacity for utter detachment, which might be described as an unconscious awareness of nothingness, of the vast gaps between the cells of the body and of the hollow core at the center of the self. Another way to say this is that deep down the unconscious mind possesses an innate, wordless understanding of the limitations of its own being, and is able to see completely under what to us is the vast submerged iceberg of the unconscious psyche. Because it is the unconscious mind itself that in a very real sense renders or generates the subjective self, on some level the unconscious must also see the limit of this self, and thus holds the keys to the deepest forms of meditative equilibrium and detachment.

14

SEXUALITY AND YOGA

There has always been a tangible mystique surrounding the deep-rooted connection between sex and yoga. Many meditators and yogis in the West were, in fact, initially drawn toward the practice of yoga precisely because of the distinctly sexual undertones that Eastern spirituality possessed, and which the blander and more puritanical Western traditions did not. The idea of yoga has often seemed to hint, almost subliminally, at immersive realms of mystical and extra-personal sexual bliss where the entranced ecstasies of spiritual union were somehow inextricably wound up with the natural sweetness and heat of sexuality. Tantra itself has become, in the modern Western lexicon, virtually synonymous with the idea of 'spiritual sexuality,' although to a certain degree this stereotype represents a misunderstanding of actual tantric philosophy. Those who have bothered to delve into the tantric literature in search of explicitly detailed yogic sex practices usually do not find them, for the simple reason that they are rarely there to be found, many of them having perhaps been purged or erased over the centuries. In any case, the direct implementation of sex into the practice of yoga, or vice versa, is more often only implied in the classical literature of Tantra, or merely hinted at in the form of sideways allegories and euphemisms.

Meanwhile, those who immerse themselves over time into the practice of yoga—hatha yoga, Kundalini yoga, tantric yoga, etc.—eventually do experience the synergic intermingling of sexuality and yoga, although not in the way a curious seeker of dark exotic Asian sex secrets might guess. At bottom yoga, like the human mind itself, is always inextricably intertwined with the physical life-force, and by extension with the psychic nectar of sexuality; the classical idea of nirvana itself has been conceptualized in terms of an ecstatic transcendental union between the cosmic principles of male and female energy, and the framework of hatha yoga possesses many techniques said to be capable of transmuting the excess sexual energy accumulated through ascetic restraint into meditative bliss and mental equanimity.

In modern times much has been said about the extended multiple ecstasies of tantric sex, our modern understanding of which is extrapolated from the ancient esoteric reaches of what has always traditionally been called the 'Left-Hand Path' of yoga; of course it is fair to say that the techniques of so-called tantric sex have very likely evolved tremendously in the past century, as they tend to be of great interest to both assiduous meditators and sexual adepts alike. Considerably less has usually been written about the fact that most flavors of traditional tantric yoga actually emphasize celibacy quite strongly. 'Brahmacarya'—sexual abstinence in body, mind and speech—is one of the five yamas listed in Patanjali's Yoga Sutras and is standard practice for most varieties of traditional Kundalini or shaktic yoga. Anybody who has visited a traditional yoga ashram will know that men and women are usually housed separately unless they are married, and are formally separated by sex during group chants and meditations; presumably this is intended to ensure a modicum of decorum, and to preclude men and women from rubbing up against each other and spontaneously beginning to 'make out' sexually as long, late night chanting sessions in darkened auditoriums begin to heat up, unlocking undercurrents of entranced sexual energy and unwinding Ego-based inhibitions and restraints. In general, sexual fraternization in a traditional ashram is usually frowned upon explicitly as a violation of ashram rules or discipline; infractions in this area are met with stern disapproval and possibly even formal reprimand or expulsion.

Many yoga gurus teach that celibacy preserves the body's strength for the practice of yoga and that 'depletion' of the body's semen, through either promiscuity or 'self-abuse,' during periods of intense meditation or sadhana can eventually weaken and harm the nervous system. The rationale for such teachings is based on the idea that the male sexual fluids are an essential component of the body's general health and vitality, with metaphysical as well as physical properties; accordingly, unless one remains celibate the practice of meditation can 'burn' or 'consume' the body's remaining vitality in a kind of 'yogic fire.' The flipside of this is the idea that if these sexual fluids are conserved and accumulated within the body they may be transmuted by the process of meditation into 'ojas,' a subtle and concentrated substance that is considered to be something like a 'liquid gold' of spiritual purity and merit. This ojas, again partly physical and partly metaphysical and perhaps even partly 'moral' in nature, is thus thought to fuel the process of meditation and spiritual progress and to nourish and purify the mind. Traditionally this is often considered to be especially important in the practice of tantric and Kundalini yoga, although there are of course many notable exceptions, in the sense that a full reservoir of stored sexual energy is thought to be essential for igniting the fire of the tantric meditation process. Just to be clear, from an atheistic and materialistic perspective there would seem to be no basis whatsoever for the idea that yoga practitioners should remain celibate or refrain from sexual activity.

At this point the objection might well be raised that the esoteric underpinnings for such rules of celibacy derive primarily from considerations of *male* physiology exclusively; although you will occasionally see a few words about the conservation of the 'female sexual fluids,' the yogic rationale for sexual prohibition seems at its root to be exclusively focused on the spiritual dangers of delinquent male ejaculation, that is, on the loss of male semen from the male body. It might in fact be said that women have been completely overlooked in the calculus that links celibacy and the conservation of sexual fluids or energy with the practice of Kundalini yoga and meditation; this is odd, unless it is merely a concealed proscription for abstinence based on some form of moral or practical reasoning. For one thing, the idea that a common principle or rule of yoga might apply so completely to one sex and not the other is incongruous with the underlying metaphysics of classical yoga, which center philosophically on the idea of an homogeneous core of divine consciousness that permeates everyone and everything alike. In fact, from the standpoint of traditional yoga philosophy one would think that there should properly be no actual differences between men and women at all: regardless of any outward differences in physical appearance, size or shape, we should expect men and women to be regarded as absolutely equal in every sense. Logically, from a mystical or metaphysical perspective if the 'spirit' (or Atman, or Buddha consciousness, etc.) is conceived of as belonging to a higher order of being than the physical body, any physical differences such as sex or race should be utterly meaningless; if we are to suppose that the universal spirit or the Atman ultimately constitutes a singular unity permeating the core of every individual alike, there should be no way that external differences between people (facial hair, sexual characteristics, skin color, etc.) could be ever regarded as anything but trivial or even illusory. In traditional yoga philosophy the condition of being either male or female is explained in terms of karma; while all conscious beings share the same fundamental essence (atman), individuals can be born as either men or women, and into various social classes and circumstances based on their past actions in previous lives; in this sense, then, men and women are somewhat interchangeable, in that men can be reborn as women and women can be reborn as men, presumably without any change whatsoever to their essential nature, according to the laws of karmic justice and reciprocation. This implies that the Hindu and Buddhist models of transmigration and reincarnation must necessarily regard men and women as absolute spiritual equals; in a superficial sense, therefore, atheistic thought dovetails nicely with Eastern spirituality on this point, since modern secular thought unequivocally regards males and females as equal in every way. Just as, from a materialistic perspective informed by the science of genetics, racism is considered grotesquely ignorant and barbaric, because there are in fact no discrete racial types or clear-cut racial divisions that exist among people, sexism too is considered primitive and unconscious, since in reality there are no differences between males and females whatsoever in terms of consciousness, mind, intellect, emotion, the nature of human experience, and so forth.

At any rate, many of the greatest masters of yoga throughout history have been female and the argument might easily be made that it is in fact females rather than males who are best suited for its practice, and are often gifted with a more natural aptitude for it. We could for instance point out that the wider female pelvis often makes it easier for women to get into the lotus position, or that women tend to be more flexible and less thickly muscled than men are. Again, though, any sexist generalizations of this sort overlook the cardinal principle that in yoga it is always the mind that is primary; since consciousness and the human mind are precisely the same in both sexes, it therefore follows that, regardless of any physical differences between them, men and women are likewise both equally suited to the practice yoga and meditation. We could go even further with this and say that a more nuanced view of the sexes might reveal that the spectrum of human sexual attributes is wide and kaleidoscopically complex, making a mockery of the simplistic and clumsy binary division of humankind into two sexes, male and female. The manifest nature and the perplexing duality of the sexes can be an endlessly enigmatic and fruitful terrain for meditative contemplation; a deeply felt understanding of the profound equality of the sexes is a doorway to tremendous insight and progress along the path of yoga. A crucial theme that deeply permeates the philosophy of esoteric tantra is that every person is in a sense a combination of both sexes, like the harmonic mix of a male and a female voice singing together; this blending of sexual characteristics and chemistries within each individual, viewable as a kind of biological anima and animus, if you will, is a central aspect of what makes us all human.

To return to the traditional yogic proscriptions for sexual abstinence, there does seem to be a kind of unwritten understanding that, in practical terms, orgasmic expenditure of sexual fluids is really only spiritually costly for *male* yoga practitioners. Whether this absurd truism stems from ancient ayurvedic notions about the vital essence of male semen, or arose over time because at some previous point in history the possibility of female yogis had been completely overlooked, is unknown. There can certainly be no doubt, however, that within spiritual and religious circles of every stripe it is invariably the males of the species who are regarded as the superstars of celibacy, and yoga ashrams, where some regard celibacy almost as a kind of macho athletic competition, are no exception. Of course, coincidentally or not, the idea that the retention of one's semen is necessary for progress on any particular spiritual path and that (male) orgasm is a disastrous waste of life-force and spiritual merit can also be useful to groups and organizations that wish to control their flocks. If males can be internally motivated to conserve their own sexual fluids, then the foxes will voluntarily guard themselves from entering the henhouse, so to speak, and most females will also thereby remain celibate by default; thus, chastity and celibacy are very likely to win the day, thereby strengthening and preserving the collective's focus on the moral object of religion or faith. Of course, if taken at face value, such a spiritual overvaluation of male semen leads logically and inexorably to an absurd zero-sum game where the spiritual merit of a lifetime could potentially be wiped out by a single sexual encounter with a female, or even worse, by succumbing to the frantically hunched and shamelessly undignified and self-defeating vice-grip of masturbation. I myself have occasionally heard seasoned male yogis describing sexually willing and available female yoginis as malicious 'semen vampires'; these men seemed to be honestly convinced that their clever, sweet and flirtatious yogic sisters, often more talented and skilled in yoga, were using their sexuality as nothing more than a sinister ruse to milk them of their precious semen, stealing their vital *shakti* or spiritual power by absorbing it into their wanton and hungrily receptive female bodies and thereby strengthening their own female shakti and bliss. Privately, some male yogis actually spoke quite seriously about this as a kind of sexual war of attrition, which women could only win through sex and men could only win through celibacy. At an unconscious level there seems to be a hint of boyish male fantasy to such notions, centering on the idea of the sexually aggressive female—the sleek and powerfully direct seductress, seething with lust and desire for the innocent male and capable of overpowering his heroic chastity and virtue, ready to squeeze it from him against his will and pull him down into the vampiric whirlpool of her own irresistible sexuality.

In any case, from the vantage point of materialism, it should be obvious that an active sex-life is not detrimental to the practice of yoga or meditation in the slightest; on the contrary, the experience of sexuality can be deeply beneficial to the practice of yoga on multiple levels. While it might at this point be a bit clichéd to say that people who practice yoga also tend to be good at sex, it is undeniable that yogic attributes such as relaxation, flexibility, muscle tone, body-awareness, mental composure, a lack of sexual inhibition and a propensity for endless repetition all translate very well into the sexual arena. Yoga improves sex and the combination of yoga and sex is capable of recharging and replenishing the body's mental and emotional systems, opening up deep circuits within the body and mind and wiring them directly into the raw current of sexuality. Such carnal adventures will certainly not be to the taste of every yoga practitioner; some, however, will find that sex can be an indispensable salvation from certain varieties of stagnant or narcissistic solipsism and can push one's meditative practice into faster and less-predictable waters, at times submerging them completely into the experience of togetherness and shared bliss or pulling them down into the hollow throbbing existential eclipse of bone-shaking orgasm. Regardless of one's personal inclinations, however, it should be unequivocally clear that there is truly nothing 'un-yogic' about sex or sexuality of any kind.

Many of the modern sexual techniques labeled as 'tantric' or 'taoist' are at their core primarily focused on coitus interruptus, or control of the male ejaculatory response in one form or another; in simplistic terms, this can generally be summed up as 'progress to orgasmic plateau, stop before you ejaculate, repeat.' These kind of techniques work by strengthening control of the muscles and nerves involved in orgasm and developing the ability to approach closer and closer to 'le petit mort' while yet managing to hold back the final uncontrolled release of orgasm and the resulting loss of sexual fluid. The female analogue for this practice is found in the extension of the female orgasmic plateau rather than in any kind of inward physical retention, as the female body is not subject to the same laws of ejaculation and recovery as that of the male. For both sexes, however, this ability to remain within the envelope of sexual arousal and stimulation for extended lengths of time can lead to something like the experience of an indefinitely prolonged orgasm, which can be intensely pleasurable and can release torrents of natural endorphins and other soothing hormones throughout the body. Yogic breath control, relaxation and meditation can also be combined with this practice of extended orgasm to great effect, and this type of sexual experience can exert pronounced inward gravitational pull toward various meditative states of mind. Having the ability to slow down and consciously experience the usually rapid, overwhelming, urgent and disorienting physical sensations of orgasm can expand one's perception of what is actually occurring in the moment, mentally and physically. In an esoteric sense, the objective is to 'merge' or absorb one's mind and consciousness into the (prolonged) experience of orgasm, combining the powerfully intoxicating physical bliss of peak sexual response with yogic body positioning, meditation and deep breathing. Some have even speculated that the experience of sexual orgasm is where the earliest yogis were first able to get a glimpse of what they imagined Samadhi might be like, a moment of absolute mental stillness or nothingness filled with a seemingly infinite inner bliss. Regardless of whether this is true or not, the modern yogi can see many parallels between the feelings and pulsations of orgasmic response and the finely tuned and exquisitely relaxed states of being encountered in deep meditation; this connection between sex and meditation is at the very crux of what we are describing as tantric or yogic sex.

Because sex presides over such a central region of the human psyche it is crucial for a practitioner of yoga to decode and untangle it's more shadowy aspects within the psyche and to be 'real' about it with oneself, so that it does not eventually become a source of negativity, repression or self-loathing; guilt-free self-acceptance and inner freedom should be embraced at every turn, as healthy and natural, and meditation requires that where dark shadows or jagged edges are encountered within the self they must be faced squarely and understood clearly. On the other hand, it would clearly be wrong to say that an active external sex life was in any way necessary for the practice of yoga; one of yoga's hidden strengths, actually, is that it can facilitate the genuine practice of celibacy (as opposed to the fake practice of celibacy). In advanced yoga practice a kind of sublimated libidinal expression may occur that can in a sense absorb or inwardly expend the pent-up flow of excess sexual energy; this can happen, for example, when deep, prolonged, repetitive stretching is combined with rigorous breath control, or during long meditation sessions in certain open-hipped seated positions. In any case, when yoga succeeds in breaking the grip of deeply ingrained muscular and emotional tensions and opening the body, it can generate feelings of physical wellbeing that are frequently described as intensely blissful and naturally intoxicating. Hatha yoga and meditation can expand awareness of the body's inner beats and rhythms in ways that can tap into complex pleasure centers within the nervous system, soothing and unwinding tension in the body with profoundly pleasurable effects. Sigmund Freud described sexual desire as a form of tension, and sexual orgasm as the release of that tension; in this sense at least it seems unavoidable that the systematic relaxation brought about by yoga must unavoidably have some degree of overlap with human sexual response in general.

There are many individuals who are naturally celibate and find perfect contentment in living their lives sexlessly, and do so without claiming 'celibacy' as an identity or making any grand show of it; true celibates express a simple asexuality that, in contrast to the flamboyant and hysterically rococo public austerity of some renunciates is effortlessly natural and unaffected. If the mind happens to lose all sexual desire and yet remains happy and content within itself, freed from the emotional eggshell of instinctive or hedonistic longing, nothing is lost; there is, if nothing else, certainly a deep freedom in asexuality and there is clearly nothing flawed or 'dirty' about it whatsoever. The essential element of real celibacy or asexuality is, however, that it must arise within a person naturally; if asexuality is imposed upon oneself out of shame or religious delusion, or as an act of submission to authority, then it is not really an authentic choice and represents merely the unfortunate walling off of the powerful living forces of sexuality from conscious expression, a jagged mental balkanization that cannot help but stultify and stiffen the entire personality.

Freeing up the mind by unlocking the physical tension stored within the body is key to the practice of yoga, and is again one of the a primary reasons that yoga is so effective in reducing stress. The hormones and parasympathetic responses of sexuality can soothe, heal and relax the body and are fully antithetical to the emotions of anxiety and stress; when meditation and yogic breathing become more sexualized, the archetypal roots of the techniques heat up naturally, and this effect can melt away stress like warm butter, generating mental bliss and liquefying any unseen icebergs of emotional tension lurking below the surface of conscious awareness. Conversely, by learning to access yogic techniques and attributes during sex a yoga practitioner also learns to access sexual responses and neurological processes during yoga and meditation; it becomes possible to elicit the sensations, rhythms, and release of sexual orgasm on a purely mental level, following the pathways of kinesthetic memory through the use of deep breathing and progressive relaxation. Because the physical sensations of sexual arousal and orgasm can be so overpowering and are so profoundly linked to the autonomic and unconscious mind they constitute a point of direct linkage between subjective consciousness and the objective physical body; therefore, by meditating directly on the feelings and pulsations of sex we gain a more direct experience of our objective selves. As the autonomic spasms of orgasm overwhelm the nervous system, the neurons of the brain light up like a vast electric swarm of sex-intoxicated honeybees, and the conscious mind dissolves for a moment into nothingness; the ability to remain within the envelope of meditation at such moments can be both incredibly lucid and tremendously pleasurable.

In some respects, the neurological stimulation that results from combining yogic techniques with the prolongation and amplification of orgasm and sexual response mirrors the symptoms of classical Kundalini awakening as they are described in Tantra; these include sexual arousal during meditation, as well as a pronounced throbbing in the sacral and genital regions; many Kundalini yoga practitioners experience a certain amount of genital 'drooling' during meditation as well as an ambient state of sexual semi-arousal that seems to extend into the spine, the shoulders, the neck and the head. The experience of unexpectedly powerful sexual fantasies during meditation is also fairly well known and in the traditional literature is explained in terms of 'samskaras' or deep memory impressions that have been activated and brought upward into consciousness by the process of meditation. Kundalini meditation can also produce a kind of mildly dissociative mental ecstasy, sometimes described metaphorically as a kind of 'yoga high,' which might best be described as an organic form of autointoxication resulting from profoundly deep physical and mental relaxation accompanied by an outpouring of natural endorphins into the body; ironically, over time these effects seem to actually increase mental focus, concentration, stamina and clarity, and have an inherently purifying effect that tends to clean out the body's adrenal fuel injectors, so to speak. Alternating physical sensations of pressure and expansiveness or hot and cold are also known to occur; mood swings and emotional surges are also not uncommon, as gridlocks of mental and physical tension are released and the psyche seeks to balance itself.

As the body progressively relaxes in this way, the nerve centers of the lower body may at times seem unusually energized or sensitive, or 'awakened' as some have described it. As a result of this increased sensitivity and responsiveness, during quiet meditation the coccyx and the lower spine may at times be felt to throb tangibly in rhythm with the heartbeat, mirroring its beats with a central pulse of neural sensitivity. In such focused states of inner quietude the pulsation of the entire body, led by the subtle thumping of the heartbeat, becomes a kind of inner mantra that one can feel emanating from the body's center outward, a natural rhythm possessing a primal soothing quality that can pull one deeper into profoundly silent meditation. Mentally focusing on what is sometimes called the 'Kundalini gland' at the very tip of the coccyx during meditation while simultaneously contracting the perineum into Mula bandha and restraining the breath with pranayama and Uddihyana bandha can create an extremely powerful meditation cocktail, which can amplify these physical sensations and drop the mind into expansive caves of deep silence. The emptiness and bliss of such states of meditation can be surprisingly intense and far more 'real' than the inexperienced meditator might imagine; it is thus to one's advantage, and this is especially true for beginners, to approach yoga meditation with patience and care and to be willing at times to simply stop and take a break for a while—sometimes for days or weeks— in order cool down and decompress, so to speak. It is also strongly recommended that one avoid the use of illicit drugs, as these can change the objective physical body and the nervous system, altering or distorting mental awareness in unseen and unpredictable ways and thereby undermining self-awareness and the process of meditation entirely. The mind, again, is always primary, and anything external required for concentration, meditation or well-being will very likely eventually prove to be an obstacle in the practice of yoga.

15

YOGIC SEX

Yogic sex combines the use of yogic techniques like asana, deep breathing, breath-retention, pratyahara and meditation with sex and lovemaking. Any additional external elements—rituals, incense, mantras, yantras, scented oils, images, music, and so forth—can be regarded as merely decorative and superficial; the actual substance of yogic sex always lies in the combination of hatha yoga and meditation with the raw energy of sex. Of course, in matters of sex there is often another meaningful factor present, which is the presence of another person with whom one is interacting on an extremely intimate and tangible level, both in a subjective sense and objectively, through direct physical contact. The presence and proximity of the 'other' during sex exerts a kind of external gravitational pull on the mind that tends to draw it away from inner meditative focus and further into the entanglements of the senses and the imagination, at times generating powerful projections of one's unconscious fantasies and desires.

In terms of raw consciousness, of course, it should not necessarily make any difference whatsoever whether one is meditating while sitting alone cross-legged on the floor or while making love with a partner on a bed; in either case, the inner experience of meditative consciousness is more or less identical. Of course, while engaged in sex with a partner one might choose to direct meditative focus outward (dharana) rather than inward (dhyana), focusing directly onto a sex partner and generating one-pointed meditation and absorption on the purely physical externalities of the lovemaking experience. Ultimately, however, even the rawest and most explicitly carnal meditation will always lead back to awareness of consciousness itself, since all sensations and perceptions, even the most explicitly sexual and intimate ones, are ultimately occurring within the mind's private theater of consciousness. Meditation, by its very nature, gradually reveals this fact.

The outward projection of meditative focus onto a sexual partner is also, in a sense, a way of 'losing oneself'—temporarily letting go of one's personal Ego-image within the imagination and supplanting it with a vivid and prolonged awareness of another person, dissolving for a while one's self-awareness into the mental image of another person. Tuning in unconditionally to a sex partner in this way—gazing into them as they gaze back into you—one may at times brush up against that which is emotionally raw or even completely irrational within them, that which is in a sense coated with what Jung called 'the slime from the depths'; this can of course be a valuable experience, certainly not to be rejected out of hand, which can be expanded and energized by a willingness to deepen the encounter outside the rules of mundane logic or rationalization. As intuition deciphers the silent Braille of a partner's unconscious sexual language, up close and in real-time, it may also inadvertently unlock and reanimate frozen fossils or relics of forgotten feelings and identities within them, obscure curios pulsing with unseen undercurrents of emotional and erotic energy that can in turn catch hold of the emotional hooks and handles within one's own mind. At times one's internal rhythms might synchronize so perfectly with those of a partner, that it may seem possible to squeeze through the slippery glass of one another's internal mental mirrors and intertwine with them directly.

In the simplest sense, yogic sex is just whatever happens when people with yoga bodies and yoga minds have sex, either with each other or with normal people. We could thus describe it as a natural manifestation of yogic attributes and insights, a natural consequence of practicing yoga over time. Sex is, of course, something profoundly physical that can exert powerful effects on the mind and the emotions, effects which can reverberate deep into the body and the psyche; it should not be surprising then that these effects might stir and awaken yogic impulses, breathing life into them as they echo through the body and mind of a yoga practitioner and rousing him or her into spontaneous meditation. What we are calling yogic sex almost always occurs spontaneously, arising, as it were, from within; nevertheless, it is worth our while here to describe a few fundamental techniques of yogic sex in rough detail. All of these techniques work because they integrate fundamental yoga practices like breath control, relaxation and meditation into the sex act, and leverage the particular advantages and strengths that yoga practitioners possess over non-yoga people. This is obviously not a comprehensive list of yogic sex techniques, but is rather merely a sampling of what we might call freeform 'kama-yoga'. All of these techniques are best initiated from within a lovemaking session already in progress, that is to say, when it just 'feels right' and the idea suggests itself to one partner or the other. It is easy to smoothly transition into any of these techniques during sex if the situation is right for it; often one is not even aware of it, but hours or days of focused yoga practice have thoroughly readied the body for the experience and as the sensations of sexual pleasure start to become more vivid and intensify, they can spontaneously pull one into the rhythms, mindsets and breathing of yoga and from there into resonant and progressively heated states of yogic bliss.

Techniques of Yogic Sex

The foundational yogic sex technique is, quite simply, to meditate during sex. This is done by relaxing the body, stilling the mind and meditatively entrancing oneself with fixation or repetition, directing one's attention inward toward consciousness and the psyche while having sex. Ideally, such meditation brings one toward an awareness of the mind's reflective nature, an awareness that the thoughts, feelings and sensations being experienced during sex are all occurring within the theater of consciousness and are thus in a sense 'made' of consciousness. The idea is to remain focused on the ineffable sensations and experience of consciousness even as orgasm overwhelms the body.

Another fundamental yogic sex technique is what could be called deep yogic sexual relaxation. This is done by deepening one's breathing and relaxing all the muscles of the body, especially the muscles of the thighs, buttocks, pelvis, and spine during sex. Yogic breathing is used to progressively relax these muscle groups and the mind is allowed to descend into the lower body, focusing conscious awareness below the navel. A transition from deep breathing to khumbaka breath retention now begins; the breath is held at intervals for a few seconds at a time before being exhaled smoothly and evenly; the lungs are then held empty for a moment before drawing in the next breath. While continuing to make love, the body is progressively relaxed further by continuing to release tension from the muscles, one muscle group or region at a time. Keep in mind that this is a freeform technique with no set pattern, sequence or structure; the idea is to follow whatever natural frequencies and rhythms the body may be suggesting and to merge and flow with those impulses and intuitions. As one's breathing becomes slower and more harmonized it is possible to notice the point where each new inhalation or exhalation arises, the top of the arc, so to speak, where an in-breath becomes an out-breath, or an out-breath becomes an in-breath; try to extend these spaces between inhalation and exhalation, allowing yourself to be absorbed into the experience. This kind of meditative breathing can be carried on during orgasm as well, by allowing the body to remain deeply relaxed, 'letting go' and releasing the muscles of the hips, pelvis, perineum and lower back, exhaling slowly as the involuntary spasms of orgasm begin to reverberate and perpetuate upward through the body; this can also be done by holding the breath in or out at the moment of climax, balancing along the edge of autonomic spasm in the silent zero instant before orgasm seizes control of the body from the inside.

Another method of blending yoga and sex could be called 'shared breathing': during sex, in any face to face or kissing position, begin to synchronize your breathing with your partner's; tune in to the rhythm of his or her inhalations and exhalations, and try to merge the rhythm of your own breathing into it. While doing this, move into progressively deeper openmouthed French kissing and, as the kissing intensifies, change the timing of your breathing so that you are inhaling when your partner exhales, drawing your partners exhalation into yourself, and then exhaling as your partner inhales, breathing into your partner with their inhalation. Continue breathing in this way and adjusting to your partner's responses as if you were sharing a single breath, passing it back and forth between one another. Be subtle yet forceful as you do this, establishing the rhythm and pace of the shared breathing and coordinating it with the rhythm of the sex act. Feel your partner's breath entering your body and imagine it moving through your spine and down into your pelvis and sacrum; try to feel a tangible connection to the deepest regions of your partner's physical being. Exhale smoothly and slowly into your partner's mouth, feeling yourself move deeper into his or her body, gradually slowing down together, lingering at the end of exhalations and savoring each subsequent inhalation with intimate abandon. Relax your mind and abandon yourself to this uninhibitedly, feeling the way your partner's body responds and pulsates with your own; try to tune-in to your partner on an unconscious level as you deepen this process, sensing through feeling and touch the presence of their unconscious mind with your own. The idea here is to try to connect with your partner on a level outside of what your senses can perceive, on an objective physical level beyond the mental abstraction of sensory perception, and to enter into a kind of 'mutual meditation' in the midst of sex.

During sex, the mind can also be focused meditatively on the 'third eye' area of the forehead, between the eyebrows. The idea is to completely concentrate one's mental attention on this area, to center one's awareness there and to in effect 'feel from' there. The technique is to keep the mind centered on the 'third eye' area as the sensations of sex arising from the lower body continue to heat up and intensify, so that the neural pulsations of sexual pleasure are felt in both the genital and the third eye area simultaneously. Ideally, this creates a kind of link between the forehead and the genital nerve complexes, so that the throb of sexual orgasm in the lower body is also mirrored within the nerves of the forehead and forebrain at the same time. This is not as strange an idea as it might seem, as sexual pleasure is in any case always experienced largely within the brain and because the forehead area between the eyes is a natural focal point of the conscious mind, which tends to be visually oriented and often expresses itself through the subtle movements of the eyebrows. While using this technique and making love it is good to relax the pelvis, especially the rear edge of the sacrum; a good practice is to imagine 'breathing into' the triangle of the tailbone and relaxing it all the way to its tip. Deep breathing can be used here to slow down the mind and relax the muscles of the pelvis, allowing for a keener awareness of the intimate connection between the head and the lower body. As orgasm approaches, try to feel the way it pulsates and moves through the genital nerve channels and up through the sacrum and the spine, and then progresses up into the head, setting up recursive, cascading waves of sensation and sexual impulse. At the peak of orgasm, the technique is to remain completely present and relaxed, meditatively focused in the forehead and the sacrum simultaneously as the neural pulsations of orgasm surge through the body and light up the circuitry of the brain.

16

BEVERLY HILLS

We leaned back into shade of the underground parking structure, basking in the summer heat still radiating from the black leather of my car's interior, our eyes drinking in the amplified darkness from beneath our sunglasses.

'When I'm in LA, sometimes I'll take a drive at rush hour for no reason,' she said. 'Just to sit in traffic and unwind.'

'When I was back East I used to fantasize during the long winters about sitting in the warm glow of California traffic,' I said. 'Ray Bans and a T-shirt, endless cars, a thick haze of smog and heat. That was my fantasy.'

She drank from her water bottle.

'Do you ever wonder if there's life on other planets?' I asked.

'The way our planet is overrun with life, how could there not be,' she said. 'It seems obvious that what we call life must be something that can occur very easily in this universe, for whatever reason. And this universe is inconceivably vast; there's something like three hundred billion stars in the Milky Way alone.'

'I do think humans will eventually colonize other planets,' I said. 'I mean, even in the next hundred years, science is going to progress so far... it's crazy. As long as we don't destroy ourselves with nuclear war, global warming, pollution, or some new fascism rip-off; which, by the way, unfortunately seems to be what a large segment of the population is unconsciously wishing for.'

'One thing I find interesting,' she said, 'Is the question of whether the more horrible and allegedly 'inhuman' aspects of our species actually stem from the animal side of our nature, or specifically from those qualities that make us most uniquely human. Or maybe they result from a deep disconnect between our neocortical faculties and our physical, animal selves.'

She drank some water.

'In some sense it's always animals, and animal nature, that suffers,' she continued. 'Even in ourselves. Think about the meat industry, the mass enslavement and slaughter of millions of animals a year. And our human indifference to animal suffering in this area can also be seen in the way we harm each other in fights, in wars, and in economic competitions. We tell ourselves that animals can't suffer because they aren't human, and so we're able to turn a blind ear to their screams of agony; but then of course during war we engage in the ruthless mass slaughter of our fellow humans, in a sense specifically because they *are* human. And maybe the reason we can do this is because we're out of touch with our common animal nature; so we can find ways to rationalize unthinkable violence and suffering even without appealing to the raw primal urgency of terror and hatred.'

I stared into a concrete corner of the parking structure.

'Humans have evolved to become partially self-aware,' she continued. 'But paradoxically they have in some sense lost touch with their more primal physical nature, and thus have also lost much of their empathy and compassion toward the animal kingdom. Humans now exploit animals on an industrial scale unimaginable even a hundred years ago, and we are now reaching a point where the entire ecosystem could conceivably collapse. Again, whether our uniquely human nature is to blame for all of this, or whether what we see in the world is just a natural animal response to being unleashed by reason, science and technology, is unclear.'

'Religious metaphysics,' she went on, 'Invariably place yet another barrier between us and our animal nature. They in effect say "you are not that"—you are not an animal—and cultivate faith in an imaginary abstraction. Of course, some traditions that emphasize reincarnation and karma do, for that reason, discourage the cruel treatment of animals; but this is always based on the implicit assumption that a human is something far greater than what an animal is, and that animals are not much more than undesirable landing spots for reincarnated souls; as if the entire animal kingdom was a kind of ironic penal colony, populated with deluded sinners fated to reincarnation into the lowly forms of animals. And, on a certain level, what difference does it make if one believes in the somewhat egotistical fantasy of having a relationship with the omniscient creator-God of the entire universe, or instead believes that the entire universe is made of God-consciousness and that it's therefore possible to merge oneself eternally into "everything"? From both perspectives the world is not much more than a spiritual test or training ground, designed to prepare one for ascension into enlightenment, with the lower animals always cast as the wretched and cautionary losers in some universal game of karma and rebirth, or sin and merit.'

'I'm not sure you're being exactly fair,' I said.

'Honestly,' she said, 'I feel that if I try to be more fair, my assessment of spiritual metaphysics will just degenerate into incoherence. For instance, if God or supreme consciousness occupies every living animal, what does it even mean to say that certain humans may be reborn as goats because of their actions in this world? Or that some may be lifted into a rapturous heaven in the 'afterlife,' while others will descend into damnation? Where does the individual mind or personality fit into all of this? The simple fact is that if humans were more in touch with their physical, animal bodies they'd be far more likely to regard themselves with compassion, and thus far more likely to treat other creatures, including other humans, with greater compassion as well.'

'But many people do have great compassion for animals,' I said. 'And I'm also sure that you're not saying that animals such as crocodiles and panthers have instinctive compassion for other animals.'

'Of course many people have tremendous compassion for animals,' she said. 'However it would be very hard to claim that we humans, as a species, are particularly compassionate toward what we regard as the lower animals. And, certainly, crocodiles and panthers are brutal, but if we humans can better understand our own brutal and predatory instincts on the level of consciousness we will be capable of that much greater empathy and self-control. The opposite is also true, that if those predatory animal instincts remain buried beneath the surface, unconscious and unseen, then they may surface unexpectedly and energetically during moments of crisis and conflict, manifesting as the evils of violence and war.'

'But then, aren't you also saying that humans are something different and apart from the animals?' I asked.

'In a sense we are, that's obvious,' she said. 'However in understanding the animal foundations of human intelligence, and the purely physical roots of our subjective consciousness, we can become more complete and integrated within ourselves, and thus better able to express our highest qualities. The animal side of human nature, in other words, is a friend, not an enemy. And this is one of the great things about yoga, that it can bring us into greater alignment with this fundamental aspect of our being.'

17

MEDITATION THEORY

In its pure form, the practice of meditation could be compared to gazing into the mind through a clear unstained window, with the essential difference being, naturally, that one can never be 'outside' of one's own mind in order to actually look 'inward.' All self-perception and self-awareness is formed of the same ineffable mind-stuff as the rest of the subjective mental world and emanates from the same field of consciousness that is the intended object of meditation. Thus, in order for meditation to be something more than sleep or an extended staring at the inner television screen of fantasy and the imagination, one must find some way to see through the inner mechanisms of mental perception in order to watch one's own mind without becoming absorbed in it.

Real meditation is always 'empty' in that it strives for clarity rather than opaqueness, and never seeks to superimpose any ideals or structures on top of self-awareness or self-perception. Real meditation should never be confused with visualization, prayer, or positive affirmation; the idea of 'guided' or 'group' meditation is, properly understood, a grotesque oxymoron and an absolute contradiction in terms. Such group techniques may be useful in various training or therapeutic contexts, but they are far different from the actual practice of yoga meditation, which is an intrinsically solitary practice. By the same token, meditation should never be preoccupied with faith or centered upon intrusive religious assumptions; any so-called 'meditation' built around religious convictions or beliefs eventually becomes little more than a struggle against reason, a battle against what is naturally unrestrained and unlimited within the mind that seeks to impose rigid structures of metaphysical belief upon it and then harden those through rationalization into 'faith.' We could liken this kind of religious 'meditation' to the act of looking through a telescope with a cartoon image of the solar system attached to its end; obviously, by looking through such a telescope one sees only the superficial picture that one has affixed to its lens and nothing more. Approaching meditation in this way converts it into the mere practice of repetitive self-indoctrination, a self-enforcing method of concentrating the mind onto what has already been swallowed and accepted as 'divine' or mystical before the process of introspection has even begun; a mechanical operation of faith rather than an open and unconditional exploration of the psyche.

Actual meditation has a dual purpose: on the one hand, it increases awareness of the self, expanding one's subjective self-image and aligning it more closely with objective reality, while on the other hand it stills and centers the mind, allowing it to find trancelike states of thought-free mental equipoise. These two objectives, which might seem like polar opposites, can and do converge in the practice of advanced meditation and an understanding of the synergy between them is key to the art of yoga. Deep yoga meditation cultivates a more direct awareness of the mind's low-level 'hardware' layer, which consists of the gross structures of the nervous system and their interfaces into the various functional components of the body. One way to picture this is to think of the 'conscious' mind as being primarily centered in the brain's neocortex, but supported and given depth and added dimension by the work of perception and processing that takes place further down inside the midbrain—within the hippocampus and the amygdala, for example. While the nervous system is only consciously aware of itself in a limited sense, the production of consciousness being essentially what we might call an autonomic process, some regions, like the neocortex, are more closely geared toward conscious thought while others function deeper within the unconscious infrastructure, the huge and heavy network of underground cables and switching stations that constitute the backbone of the entire organism. There are levels of will and consciousness within the psyche that exist outside of what is normally accessible by the conscious mind, which are not connected to the verbal centers of the brain and can only make themselves heard indirectly, through the seemingly random interactions of consciousness with imagination, perception and memory. Evidence of such interactions can be seen in the appearance of a sandwich or a taco in the imagination when one is hungry, for instance, or in the semiconscious neural tingle that tells one it is time to urinate. There are endless interactions between the verbal and the nonverbal aspects of the self, and in fact it is not a tremendous leap to say that there is essentially no rigid barrier or distinction between the conscious and the unconscious mind. As consciousness or awareness expands in the practice of meditation it must necessarily venture further into the regions of what is unconscious or subconscious; in yoga, one way this is done is to extend awareness and conscious control deeper into the physical structure of the body, into the undecipherable, sealed off and locked areas of the nervous system—the midbrain, the basal ganglia, the spinal cord, etc.—that are normally well outside of conscious awareness yet still exist on the same biological 'grid' as consciousness, and always in direct connection with it.

To draw an analogy from computer science, we might say that information is 'coded' with a different (hardwired) 'language' or protocol within the spine or the basal ganglia than it is within the neocortex; this is analogous to the low-level 'machine language' that a computer uses to interact with its structural electronic components, as compared with the high-level languages that programmers generally use, or the even more simplified and abstracted scripting languages and graphical interfaces designed for consumers or end-users. Somebody may, for example, use HTML to place graphics on a web page, but have no understanding whatsoever of the internal mechanics of the underlying rendering software or the graphics card components that do the low-level heavy lifting of displaying digital images on various types of computer screens. Within the human body, various low-level subsystems for encoding and relaying information within the organism may have remained virtually unchanged across tens of millions of years of evolution, constituting a kind of link from the conscious mind back to its primeval roots. According to the Triune Brain theory, these older and more primitive structures of the brain stem and the so-called limbic system form a kind of foundation upon which the higher structures and cognitive faculties of the neocortex have been built by evolution; this inner core of the brain and the nervous system manages all of the body's vital autonomic functions and forms the substrata of physical awareness in which abstract consciousness and the sense of individual existence is rooted. This multilayered structure of the nervous system of course has many implications for how we perceive the world and ourselves; the amygdala and the hippocampus, for example, routinely intercept sensory data from the eyes and ears before it reaches the neocortex or the conscious mind, and can initiate feelings and responses through a kind of unconscious 'preprocessing' that can directly determine the content and direction of conscious thought.

Here again the yogic concept of quieting or 'stilling' the mind comes into play; through meditation, it is possible to temporarily silence all abstract verbal thought and turn the mind's attention inward, with the aim of perceiving the physical body directly, from inside. If the yoga practitioner is able to, in some sense, unlock these more primitive parts of the nervous system, a door can be opened to experiencing a certain reptilian quality of mental stillness, a primal organic trance centered in the body's natural rhythms; this taps into an unfathomably ancient animal equipoise that far predates abstract thought and is directly linked to the raw physical sense of being that constitutes the depth and underlying 'realness' of consciousness and the individual sense of self. Focusing the mind inward in order to develop the connection between consciousness and the physical body is pure yoga, and progresses toward an ability to link consciousness downward into the body through the low-level core of the nervous system; using the techniques of yoga in this way develops deeper and more profound levels of body-awareness, while exploring the body's fundamental unity with the mind.

Human consciousness tends to be oriented toward visual and verbal processing. The mind generally orients itself visually, and communicates with itself as well as others through words; internally, the mind 'sees' abstract concepts in images, and relentlessly labels and describes everything it encounters with words, 'talking' to itself and 'listening' to its own thoughts. The practice of meditation, however, in that it enables a kind of 'descent' into the more primitive aspects of the psyche, opens one to a more direct kinesthetic awareness of the physical self, and thereby also to a greater awareness of the intuitive signals sent by the adaptive unconscious; a heightened sense of how a particular situation 'feels,' for instance, or the occasional ability to 'taste' in a sip of tea what a friend might be feeling. By learning to commune with the low-level core of the nervous system one is able to experience a more comprehensive unity of the self, accessing one's unconscious 'horse sense' or innate animal wisdom, and bringing one's thoughts and feelings into smoother alignment with each other. Symbolically, the reptilian inner core of the Triune Brain, which emerges out of the black-sheathed primordial cable of the spine and sits atop it like sealed bulb, might be represented as a kind of inner cobra; this image, obviously drawn from Tantra, is also found in hatha yoga: in Naga asana, the cobra pose, as the spine flexes and peels itself upward from the ground and the head rises toward the sky like the hood of a cobra, one's mental awareness properly remains focused within this living bulb of the brainstem.

As the mind in meditation rubs up against the outer edges of consciousness, it is the nervous system itself that is eventually felt to be the barrier or limitation to self-awareness, difficult to perceive directly precisely for the reason that it is also the physical object generating all subjective or abstract awareness. In yoga meditation, this subjective limitation of consciousness—the fact that one cannot 'feel' or experience beyond the physical structure of the nerves or the brain—leads one to seek further inward in order to find balance and solidity amidst the vast sea of unknowable chaos outside. The living frontier of the unconscious mind comes into play here as well, it being the abyss that stares back into one, at times choosing to reveal to the conscious mind obscure and long-forgotten passageways and chambers within the brain, which can lead to unique insights about the self or to more direct internal perception and control of the body.

If meditation is practiced consistently, eventually the mind's attention becomes increasingly drawn toward the phenomena of consciousness itself. Having once truly 'noticed' the existence of consciousness, a meditator gradually finds it to be always present, at every moment of every minute of every hour, never out of view if looked for and yet continually unexplained and continually the entry point into an open and unresolved riddle. Meditation can clear the way for occasional moments of startling clarity when the mind might catch a glimpse of consciousness directly before it slips away again, disappearing into the seemingly inert bedrock walls of one's inner theater. Flashes of reflective self-awareness, the occasional catching of the mind's eye gazing back at one in the mental mirror of meditation, can begin to subtly change one's sense of self and of existence, gradually developing into what eventually becomes an intoxicating fascination, the beginnings of what we could describe as an 'addiction' to meditation.

Meditation is, by its very nature, a wholesome addiction that is not reliant upon anything outside of itself or outside of the body; it can be supremely relaxing and restorative and having once genuinely tasted it, the mind reliably begins to crave it. Meditation is also a self-sustaining practice, in that it generates a genuine and lasting sense of contentment that feeds back into the essence of the practice itself; a little bit of real meditation goes a very long way indeed, often carrying unexpected and mind expanding insights that can in turn make future meditation sessions even deeper and easier. It may seem paradoxical, but an experienced meditator can easily go weeks or even months without properly sitting for meditation at all, being perfectly content to savor past memories and experiences of meditation; conversely, when meditation feels more in season the same yogi might meditate relentlessly for days at a time, remaining inwardly immersed to the exclusion of all other activities.

A key point here is that real meditation is never something robotic or mechanical, and is never the product of structure or routine; genuine meditation comes from within, and always has its roots in inner freedom. Experienced yogis find that meditation eventually comes knocking of its own accord; the external practice of what passes for meditation from the outside can at best only set the stage for its actual inner substance. Ultimately, what can be perceived in meditation is only what the mind is willing to reveal to itself; it is therefore always essential to trust and love the mind in order to meditate well.

18

MEDITATION TACTICS

The physical, animal body is what gives consciousness its depth and its solid, tangible core of identity and selfness; the role the body plays in meditation, therefore, simply cannot be overstated. A relaxed, comfortable and well-oxygenated body is essential to the process of meditation, and it is the physical suppleness, intuition and body-control developed in the practice of hatha yoga that brings meditation into the domain of the real. Hatha yoga develops body-consciousness and the ability to release tension and relax physically; these twin attributes, when combined with an understanding of posture and position, make it far easier to immerse oneself in long, detached meditation sessions without getting distracted by physical discomfort. If the body is positioned awkwardly or unevenly during meditation, various joints, nerves and muscles may begin to strain or ache after a while, something that can nibble at the edges of one's awareness and gradually pull the mind out of meditation. All of the various crossed legged upright-seated positions are fine for relaxed meditation, and most reclining or supine lying positions are also good; the floor, a couch, or a comfortable chair can easily be augmented with strategically placed cushions to create a firm and supportive nest for meditation, which makes it easy for the pelvis and spine to open and elongate. Many of the 'restorative' yoga postures that are frequently taught in modern yoga classes are also quite suitable for meditation, and can be personalized and augmented for a luxurious experience. A comfortable yet open and extended position allows one to relax deeply and to consciously transition into meditation without curling into an inert cocoon of sleep. That the body's position must be 'open' is an absolutely crucial detail here; however one may be sitting, reclining or lying for meditation, the femurs should be rotated outward, opening the hips. The spine should be lengthened, and the shoulders should be rolled back slightly, opening the collarbones and the chest; the palms should face upward, rotating the upper arms outward. This type of position is conducive to conscious awareness and concentration, and yet is also in a sense passive and vulnerable; some people do experience a certain level of anxiety or uneasiness in these kind of wide-open positions, however in order to truly let go of deep tension it is necessary to let go of the body's defensive reflexive tightness, and therefore any resistance to relaxing or meditating in an 'unprotected' position like this should be worked through.

An interesting thing about deep relaxation is that it can at times evoke feelings of fear, anxiety and emotional pain. This actually happens precisely because one is letting go of accumulated tension; this tension is, subconsciously, often felt to protect one from danger, either real or imaginary, or from previous emotional pain. 'Inner resistance' to meditation is something that can at times feel alarmingly real as wide-open relaxation begins to descend; an unnamed itch of anxiety can suddenly come upon one, as relaxation unearths unseen undercurrents of emotion and stress. The ever-vigilant mechanisms of the 'fight-or-flight' stress response can resist and push back against the advancing tide of relaxation, holding onto muscular tension that unconsciously serves as a kind of emotional armor protecting the body and Ego from the outside world. The sudden absence of this ambient tension can make one feel disoriented and emotionally vulnerable, a sensation sometimes experienced as a kind of falling or weightlessness, as if the floor had suddenly vanished from beneath one. During the brief supine meditation session at the end of a hatha yoga class one can occasionally hear this occurring: one of the students in the darkened room will suddenly gasp and suck in a startled panic-breath as if they'd just caught themselves from falling, frantically pulling their way out of meditation as if to grab back onto their comfortable shell of physical tension.

The borderline at the edge of truly deep relaxation is precisely where one must have the courage and determination to fully relinquish one's thoughts, worries and emotions in order to surrender to the expansive parasympathetic openness of meditation. A key point to remember is that on some level physical tension only exists because one is holding on to it, and (unconsciously) refuses to let go of one's own grip upon it; ultimately, one creates and holds onto one's own physical tension—no one else can exert direct control over this. As these self-inflicted unconscious chokepoints of stress and tension begin to unlock and open up during meditation, the challenge can often be to confront, accept and defuse the toxic emotional residues that are released. This is where detachment is crucial, allowing one to stay mentally present and to continue meditating freely in the current moment, even while fully aware that there might be a lot of thinking and analytical homework to be done later. Again, physical position is crucial; notice that the type of relaxation described here is far different from, for example, curling up under a blanket and falling asleep, or having a few drinks and watching TV. Although somewhat relaxing, these kinds of cozy nesting behaviors tend to insulate and protect one from underlying tensions and existential anxieties while at the same time actively distracting the mind— almost the precise opposite of what is required for meditation. Of course, it is not altogether unusual to fall asleep during meditation; this can sometimes happen for a few minutes right at the start of a session. Many yoga practitioners have had the experience of sitting down to meditate and falling asleep almost immediately, only to awaken sometime later seated in the same spot, immersed in lucid and expansive meditation, the brain having spontaneously 'rebooted' itself within an abbreviated sleep cycle and transitioned seamlessly into meditation of its own accord.

The essential technique of meditation is to be fully present with oneself, remaining inwardly focused on the psyche without getting caught up and absorbed into one's thoughts, memories, perceptions and daydreams. The idea is to turn consciousness onto itself, turning away from the projection screen of one's imagination in order to gaze into the source and substance of thought itself. To meditate in this way one's mental attention must be focused on the mind itself, while staying detached from the content or meaning of particular thoughts; the persistent and reflexive impulse to become absorbed in imagination and internal self-talk is sidestepped by a progressively stronger awareness of the mind-stuff from which all thoughts are formed, the conscious and reflective medium of consciousness itself. The key lies in being able to detach oneself in meditation from the catchy narrative flow of thought, the interlaced and interlinked flow of imagination, fantasy and inner dialogue that always seems to be one step ahead of self-awareness.

When the mind seems to 'push back' against the process of meditation, and one finds oneself repeatedly absorbed within the narrative matrix of thought and continually 'forgetting' to meditate from one instant to the next, a good practice is to simply notice what thoughts 'look like'; in the case of daydreams and fantasies, try to mentally focus on them and to 'see' them more clearly. Minus the will or wish to indulge in them, one's mental simulacra often evaporate like mirages. An excellent and highly advanced meditation technique is to simply watch oneself 'fail' at meditation; since such failures are so marvelously reliable one has ample opportunity to witness its mechanics repeatedly in real-time. Each successive moment that meditation is abandoned and the mind begins to be ensnared once again in thought there is yet another opportunity to witness the minute event of a new thought rising up within the current instant of time.

Deep physical and mental relaxation is vital to the meditation process. Progressively deeper levels of physical relaxation, relaxation upon relaxation, allows one to unlock unconsciously held mental and physical tension, and thus frees the mind up for clear and unhindered introspective awareness. Such ultra-relaxation, combined with meditative concentration and awareness, can generate intensely pleasurable sensations of physical and mental bliss. In some states of deep relaxation the metronome of the heart can be felt subtly throbbing through the spine, nerves and brain; following or 'tuning in' to these subtle layers of rhythmic throb and pulse tends to soothe and entrance the mind, unlocking expansive chambers of meditative space inside. Such states of supple meditative stillness also give one a much more delicate sense of where physical and emotional tension is impeding circulation in the body by constricting blood vessels and tightening skeletal muscles; as kinesthetic sensitivity increases, one can easily notice areas of tension and tightness through a certain 'stuck' feeling, or the dull ache of localized hypoxia. By focusing mental awareness directly on such trouble-spots and combining it with deep breathing and progressive relaxation, many of the knots and roadblocks of deep tension or stress can be untangled easily, which in turn opens the way for deeper and more serene meditation.

In meditation, one should gradually develop a stronger kinesthetic 'X-ray' sense, if you will, of what the body is feeling; one way to improve this kind of kinesthetic insight is to focus directly on tension or pain when it is present, clarifying in the mind its precise physical location. Rather than settling for fuzzy approximations—a vague cloudy sensation of discomfort in a generalized area of the body, for example—the mind should attempt to zero-in on the precise source of the problem, expanding subjective awareness of its location and nature.

Moving directly toward pain, toward the body's epicenters of tension and discomfort rather than away from them, is an advanced trick of yoga meditation. When tension can be isolated in three-dimensional space, it is possible to get a conscious 'grip' on it, making it far easier to unlock and release. Because a lot of muscular tension is held within the body unconsciously, simply developing a deeper awareness of a particular body area and a more accurate 'feel' for it can begin to dissolve and unwind tension there immediately. In meditation, try to mentally trace and follow muscles back to their associated bones, tendons and ligaments, inwardly searching for interconnections and relationships; allow joints to open and muscles to lengthen and relax, using deep breathing persistently to unlock tension wherever it is found. Applied diligently, this kind of relaxation can smooth away deeply ingrained negative emotions, and can heal some of the painful emotional scars that tension has etched into the body's muscles and neural pathways.

If we consider yoga meditation carefully, we can see in it various elements and characteristics of what in the West is often called trance or hypnosis. There has, in fact, long been a certain connection in the Western imagination between yoga and hypnotism: the Indian snake charmer, the ascetic yogi lying peacefully on a bed of nails, the turbaned mystic with the power of mind-control, and so forth. In any event, the fact is that many forms of yoga meditation do indeed incorporate trance and hypnosis in one form or another, and this turns out to be a very interesting and powerful aspect of esoteric yoga technique.

When Patanjali's classic definition of yoga as 'the stilling of the thought-waves of the mind' is reframed into a modern materialistic context that includes the existence of the unconscious mind, it can easily be interpreted as describing a form of self-hypnotic trance. This 'stilling' of the 'thought-waves,' whether it is conceptualized as using one-pointed mental focus and attentional absorption to quiet the mind, or in terms of slowing the mind down by making its thoughts more uniform and repetitious, bears an unmistakable similarity to various modern techniques of hypnosis. Looking deeper into Patanjali's Yoga Sutras, we find additional clues and similarities:

3.1 "Dharana (concentration) is the fixation of the mind on a singular point."

3.2 "In this concentration, the flow of focused attention and uniform thought is called dhyana, or meditation."

3.3 "When the mental image of the object of meditation is all that is present in the mind, and the mind is not even aware of itself, this is called Samadhi (one-pointed or single-minded concentration)."

3.4 "When these three are combined in focus upon the same object simultaneously, this is called Samyama (total mental absorption)."

Assuming, as we do, the existence of the Freudian and the post-Freudian unconscious mind, which obviously had not yet been articulated in the age of Patanjali, the forms of mental absorption described in these sutras clearly imply a form of self-directed trance, as the intentional cessation of conscious thought will necessarily bring the unconscious mind to the forefront of awareness. In another chapter, Patanjali has gone even further in this direction:

1.38 "By meditating on the form and content of dream imagery, or on the nature of deep dreamless sleep, the mind of the yogi becomes still."

By focusing the mind intensely on remembering one's dreams, various doors to the unconscious mind may be opened in much the same way they are inside of hypnotic trance; the symbolism of one's dreams also tends to be amplified by this extra attention, as the conscious mind becomes further attuned to the feelings of the unconscious self. The strengthening of this bond between the conscious and the unconscious is one of the key elements of hypnosis. Similarly, by meditating on the state of deep dreamless sleep, one is applying hypnotic technique in the most literal sense, eliciting trance by retracing one's steps back into the subconscious domain of sleep itself.

An occasional discrete droplet of direct hypnotic autosuggestion can also be effective in meditation, so long as the unconscious is approached with love and respect, as being the root of consciousness and the mind, rather than a rented mule or some dumb mechanical device to be shouted at or programmed. The unconscious is, after all, joined at the hip with the psyche, and inseparable from the body; extending compassion and care toward this often mute and hidden aspect of oneself is, therefore, an essential expression of self-love.

In the right spots, hypnotic suggestion can be very effective for deepening and prolonging meditation or for transitioning into yoga-nidra (yogic sleep); this effectiveness of hypnotic suggestion springs from the peculiar ability of the human mind to act 'as if' and willingly suspend disbelief, accepting for a time something unreasonable and nonlinear into its subjective map of reality. There is no real danger in this, so long as the bargain one is making with oneself is properly understood; autosuggestion requires a conscious and deliberate suspension of disbelief, which allows one to accept an assertion or suggestion at face value and to proceed as if it were objectively true; in meditation this might take the form of something like 'I am now going into deep meditation,' or 'I am now relaxing deeply and letting go of the tension in my muscles.' Again, in order to be effective such autosuggestions should be visualized, 'felt' and intuitively understood; their effectiveness will always depend on clear intention and inner direction rather than on verbal messaging or cumulative repetition. A purely verbal suggestion might be interpreted in many different ways by the unconscious mind or ignored altogether if it is not grounded in feeling or vivid conception; unless one has had the experience of meditation, for example, how could simply telling oneself to meditate again and again reliably lead one toward the correct destination? But if the mind can be focused, as Patanjali suggests, on memories of the sleep state—or, for that matter on the remembered sensations of sexual orgasm, deep meditation or trance—it then has a clear path for eliciting that particular frame of mind. When this slight nudge of autosuggestion is combined with one-pointed meditative concentration and sensory withdrawal, it can be phenomenally effective for rapidly deepening meditation, bringing the various levels of the psyche into alignment and unifying their resources around the singular intention to relax and meditate.

In a certain sense, the conscious mind is centered in the area of the eyes and forehead; this area is thus a good starting point for transitioning into hypnotic or meditative trance. This is done by strongly relaxing the eyes and all the facial muscles around them, and allowing the eyelids to passively lock themselves closed as the eyeballs pull back into the eye sockets. The eyelids should feel as if sealed or glued shut and a slight upward rotation into the skull should accentuate each eyeball's gentle inward vacuum tug. The neck should lengthen, as if toward the crown of the head, and one's breathing should be slow and nasal, felt to swell and occupy the forehead sinuses. At this point in the technique, a hypnotic autosuggestion maybe be given silently and inwardly—preferably something simple such as 'I am now going into a deep trance,' or 'I am now going into the state of deep meditation.' The suggestion itself need only be repeated once; what matters here is a unity of intention and a willingness to temporarily suspend disbelief and simply assume the desired outcome (in this case meditation or trance) as a matter of fact. To further deepen this kind of hypnotic trance various mental devices can be used, such as counting backward from ten to zero or imagining oneself descending into a dark hole at the base of one's imagination. From that point one should simply continue to relax progressively deeper while meditating on consciousness and the presence of the psyche.

Again, a crucial aspect of such techniques lies in making a kind of deal with oneself to accept something uncritically, proceeding 'as if' a desired outcome were certain or had already occurred in order to enlist the resources of the unconscious will and the imagination; we can certainly draw some parallels here to the Zen concept of 'doing without doing.' Clearly, an 'action' such as falling asleep requires a certain letting go or relinquishment of intention and active doing. One does not actively 'go' to sleep; instead, one releases one's grasp on wakefulness and sleep comes of its own accord; thus, one essentially 'does' (go to sleep) without 'doing.' This is unavoidable, since sleep is not an action but a mental state that is mediated by the objective physical brain out of the view of conscious awareness. Thus, the Zen construct of 'doing without doing' can be understood logically, not as anything mystical or inscrutably paradoxical, but rather as a pointer to a broader conception of the self, the greater part of which must necessarily be outside of subjective consciousness at any given moment.

The use of mantra repetition in meditation and trance is a very ancient practice, the origins of which are buried deep in prehistory. For the modern practitioner, mantra repetition—the silent inward chanting or repetition of a word or phrase—can in fact be a very useful tool for meditation, so long as it is clearly understood that no word or mantra actually can possess any 'magical' or mystical power beyond what people themselves may give it, and the practice is employed solely for its repetitive metronomic qualities and its utility as an object of inward mental focus. The Sanskrit term 'mantra' literally means 'word,' i.e., a structure of letters representing a sound or a sequence of sounds, which corresponds to a particular meaning. Mental mantra repetition, or japa, is based on the idea that during inward repetition a word possesses a kind of 'sound' or 'vibration' within the mind, in the same way that one can in a sense 'hear' certain types of thoughts, for example the memory or repetition of a song inside one's head; by repeating a single word or phrase in the stillness of meditation, its mental 'sound,' if you will, comes to be perceived more distinctly, as a kind of pulsation within the mind. Mantra repetition can be used as a tool for quieting and focusing the mind, which can temporarily reduce the variance and fluctuation of one's thoughts; monotonous mental repetition can essentially displace all other verbal mental content and generate a kind of steady mental uniformity of thought. Mantra repetition is also a useful way in meditation for observing the inner mechanisms of the mind itself; when the mind is engaged in the repetition of a single predictable thought it's much easier to meditatively 'step outside' of the thinking process and focus attention directly on the substance and origin of thought. Again, when the mind gets caught up into its thoughts, fantasies and memories during meditation it in effect ceases to be aware of itself and loses the thread of sustained conscious self-awareness.

The repetition of a single word within the mind becomes increasingly predictable and uniform and a meditator can use this predictable uniformity to detach from and step outside of the subjective narrative of thought in order to see the mind more clearly in real-time. A meditator can eventually anticipate each fresh mantra repetition and thus has a window of chance to observe its emergence from the unconscious mind, as well as its sound and shape and the ineffable sense in which it is reflected within consciousness. Oftentimes, whether one is engaged in meditation or not, multilayered waves of thought and imagination can be found to have arrived well ahead of any self-conscious awareness of the fact; one's intimate engagement with these sequences of mentation essentially 'protects' one from self-awareness, and constitutes a kind of continual prophylactic forgetfulness, which cloaks the presence of the psyche from conscious awareness. Through the strategy of mantra repetition, however, a baseline of control and predictability within the mind can be established during meditation, which in turn can facilitate more direct observation of the substance and mechanism of thought, and allow one to look further into its root source in the unconscious.

Vasugupta, the ancient writer of the Shiva Sutras, wrote that 'Cittam mantraha': 'Mind is mantra.' The meaning of this aphorism is that the conscious mind tends to assume the form of whatever thoughts or images it is occupied with and that therefore when the mind is occupied with the letters and sounds of a mantra it in a sense assumes their form. The inverse of this is also implied by the aphorism, in that during inward repetition of a mantra its inner 'sound' or vibration necessarily takes shape wholly within the substance of the mind, and thus each subjective instance of the mantra consists of mind and nothing else. This phenomenon is easily observable whenever one visualizes or imagines any object, as the mind forms and holds a mental image of the object within itself while simultaneously 'seeing' or perceiving it. When one becomes absorbed in the content and storyline of one's thoughts, daydreams and memories, this is what Vasugupta describes as incorrectly identifying oneself with the content or meaning of thought; what he prescribes instead is to meditate upon one's thoughts directly regardless of their form or content, or their particular value along any subjective qualitative spectrums between 'purity' and 'filth' or 'goodness' and 'badness,' etc. Every structure of thought and imagination created within the mind consists, at bottom, only of the mind itself; thus, by meditating directly upon any thought whatsoever, one is in effect meditating directly upon the mind and upon the ephemeral pulsations of subjective consciousness within it. This is a quintessentially yogic approach to meditation.

In a very real sense, then, a meditation session is never the time to suppress, silence or control one's thoughts, but is rather an opportunity to observe them within their natural habitat, which is consciousness. One's thoughts and internal mental images, observed clearly from a perspective of detachment, necessarily reveal at every instant the shimmering presence of the psyche itself. This style of meditation is enormously effective because, rather than fighting against the action and energy of the mind, the meditator simply seeks to 'rise above' and observe its manifestations from a more stable vantage point. This completely obviates the necessity of struggling to suppress, censor or purify one's thoughts, as every thought becomes itself an object of meditation, and what was formerly an obstacle now reveals itself to be pure psyche, all of its distant horizons existing nowhere but within the self, melting and transforming into endless permutations of consciousness.

Mantra repetition can be a valuable meditation tool for several reasons, beginning with the fact that its sheer repetitiveness can soothe and center the mind, clearing away and dissolving circular logic or emotionally jagged or compulsive trains of thought, thus allowing one to get down to the meditative process of relaxation and detached introspection. The mental action of mantra repetition occupies the verbal thinking mechanism of the mind and unifies it in focus upon a singular object, the mantra, thus fueling what Patanjali describes as a 'steady wave of concentration'; this trancelike uniformity of thought can create a kind of mental stillness or equilibrium, allowing the mind's eye to turn inward. Thus, mantra repetition can be a useful tool for generating the mental steadiness and inner resolve that yoga practitioners have traditionally been known for. The basic technique for using mantra repetition in meditation is to repeat a word mentally, thinking or intoning it silently to oneself at a relaxed, consistent pace; this is often synchronized with the breathing, the word being inwardly repeated once on the in-breath and once on the out-breath. As for the selection of a particular mantra, virtually any single word or short simple sequence of words will do fine; again, what is relevant here is not the content of any particular words but rather the mechanism of introspective repetition itself. Made-up nonsense words, in fact, probably make the best mantras, because they carry no extraneous 'baggage' of linguistic meaning or association; an excellent way create a unique mantra is to simply combine the names of various letters from the English alphabet into two or three-syllable combinations. The combination 'L-M-N' might thus be intoned 'el-em-en,' and the combination 'Z-D-M,' might be intoned 'zee-dee-em,' and so forth.

Bibliography

Aranya, Hariharananda Swami and Mukerji, P.N. *Yoga Philosophy of Patanjali.* State University of New York Press, 1983.

Avalon, Arthur. *The Serpent Power.* Dover Publications, 1974.

Burley, Mikel. *Classical Samkhya and Yoga: An Indian Metaphysics of Experience.* Routledge, 2006.

Cassirer, Ernst. *An Essay on Man.* Doubleday Anchor Books, 1953.

Feuerstein, Georg. *The Shambhala Encyclopedia of Yoga.* Shambala, 2000.

Freud, Sigmund and Strachey, James. *The Ego and the Id.* W.W. Norton and Company, 1989.

Freud, Sigmund and Strachey, James. *The Interpretation of Dreams.* Discus Books, 1967.

Freud, Sigmund. *New Introductory Lectures on Psychoanalysis.* Penguin Books, 1973.

Freud, Sigmund. *The Unconscious.* Penguin Books, 2005.

Gray, Henry. *Gray's Anatomy: The Classic Collector's Edition.* Garmercy, 1988.

Iyengar, B.K.S. *Light on the Yoga Sutras of Patanjali.* Thorsons, 2002.

Iyengar, B.K.S. *Light on Yoga.* George Allen and Unwin, 1965.

Jung, C.G. and Shamdasani, Sonu. *The Psychology of Kundalini Yoga.* Princeton University Press, 1996.

Korzybski, Alfred. *Science and Sanity.* The International Non-Aristotelian Library Publishing Company, 1948.

Lacan, Jacques and Fink, Bruce. *Ecrits: The First Complete Edition in English.* W.W. Norton and Company, 2007.

Larson, Gerald James. *Classical Samkhya: An Interpretation of its History and Meaning.* Ross-Erickson, 1979.

Ledoux, Joseph. *The Emotional Brain: The Mysterious Underpinnings of Emotional Life.* Simon and Schuster, 1998.

Mencken, H.L. *The Philosophy of Friedrich Nietzsche.* Kessinger Publishing, 2007.

Mishra, Kamalakar. *Kashmir Shaivism: The Central Philosophy of Tantrism.* Rudra Press, 1993.

Nietzsche, Friedrich and Hollingdale, R.J. *Beyond Good and Evil.* Penguin Classics, 2003.

Olivelle, Patrick. *Pancatantra, The Book of India's Folk Wisdom.* Oxford University Press, 1997.

Olson, Carl. *Original Buddhist Sources: A Reader.* Rutgers University Press, 2005.

Osho. *Sex Matters: From Sex to Superconsciousness.* St. Martin's Griffin, 2002.

Reich, Wilhelm. *Character Analysis.* Farrar, Straus and Giroux, 1980.

Robinson, Paul. *The Freudian Left.* Harper Colophon Books, 1969.

Sagan, Carl. *Contact.* Orbit & Abacus, 1997.

Saraswati, Satyananda Swami. *Kundalini Tantra.* Yoga Publications Trust, 1984.

Schopenhauer, Arthur and Hollingdale, R.J. *Essays and Aphorisms.* Penguin Classics, 1973.

Schopenhauer, Arthur and Payne, E.F.J. *The World as Will and Representation, in Two Volumes.* Dover Publications, 1966.

Swami Svatmarama. *The Hatha Yoga Pradipika.* Forgotten Books, 2008.

Tallis, Frank. *Hidden Minds: A History of the Unconscious.* Arcade Publishing, 2002.

Thompson, Hunter S. *Fear and Loathing in Las Vegas.* Modern Library, 1996.

von Franz, Marie-Louise. *Archetypal Dimensions of the Psyche.* Shambala, 1999.

Watson, Craig. *Basic Human Neuroanatomy.* Little, Brown and Company, 1991.

Wilson, Timothy. *Strangers to Ourselves: Discovering the Adaptive Unconscious.* Belknap Press of Harvard University, 2004

www.ingramcontent.com/pod-product-compliance
Lightning Source LLC
Chambersburg PA
CBHW060132100426
42744CB00007B/760